Elbows off the Table,
Napkin in the Lap,
No Video Games During Dinner

▸◂

Elbows off the Table,

Napkin in the Lap,

No Video Games During Dinner

THE MODERN GUIDE TO TEACHING CHILDREN
Good Manners

Carol McD. Wallace

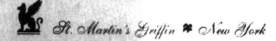 *St. Martin's Griffin* ❦ *New York*

Design by Judith Stagnitto Abbate

Library of Congress Cataloging-in-Publication Data

Wallace, Carol.
    Elbows off the table, napkin in the lap, no video
games during dinner : the modern guide to teaching
children good manners / by Carol McD. Wallace.—1st
ed.
        p.   cm.
    ISBN: 978-0-312-14122-6
    ISBN: 0-312-14122-X
    1. Etiquette for children and teenagers.   I. Title.
BJ1857.C5W29   1996
395'.122—dc20   95-43788
                                                   CIP

P 1

To William and Timothy, who want everyone to know that they aren't perfect either,

and to my mother-in-law Peggy, who did such a good job with Rick

Acknowledgments

My mother started it all, of course, and I have to thank her for the confidence to manage almost any social situation, as well as a thorough grounding in thank-you notes.

I would never have dreamed of writing about manners if I hadn't spent hours and hours studying manuals by Letitia Baldridge, Marguerite Kelly, Judith Martin and Marjabelle Young Stewart. To that foundation I have added a great deal of advice from friends and relatives, including Barbara Butler, Lisa Callahan, Nancy Casserley, Clarice Cole, Pat Emery, Wendy Hilboldt. Laura Lloyd, Nanci McAlpin, Gioia Pastre, and Eve Wallace.

And this information would never have made it into book form without the ever-stalwart help of my agent Lynn Seligman, and the faith and vision of my editor Hope Dellon and her colleague Jenny Notz.

Contents

Elbows off the Table,
Napkin in the Lap,
No Video Games During Dinner

➤◄

Introduction

Most parents would like their children to have good manners. Who wouldn't want to hear "Please" and "Thank you" at dinnertime, and have the door held open by a small person in sneakers? Certainly we all hope that as adults our children will be comfortable and self-possessed in a range of circumstances. The French term *savoir-faire* perfectly expresses the notion of knowing how to do things in different situations.

But the very idea of teaching manners causes a lot of anxiety, and for good reasons. We all feel overburdened: Surely manners can wait until we get Johnny potty trained/reading/into college. Everyday discipline is hard enough to manage. Who would be fool enough to add all this extra behavior that has to be monitored? We need to teach our children the skills that will help them cope in the world, and manners often don't seem that important.

I believe, though, that good manners are an *essential* part of our children's education. Behaving courteously to the people around you is a skill, too. And it's important for a basic, if cynical, reason: People with good manners are more likely to get what they want. Imagine this scenario: There are two children in your kitchen. One says, "Mrs. Parker, could I have a glass of juice, please?" (This is well within the capability of the average five-year-old). The other says, "I want some juice," and tries to grab the cup from your hand. Which kid is going to get her juice first?

This example also points out something important about manners: *They have to be taught.* It's all very well to believe that a child's innate good nature will make her behave lovably. But this simply isn't true. A large proportion of manners—particularly those concerning eating—involves going against your instincts. Waiting to be served, waiting to eat, tasting things you don't like the looks of, taking small bites and chewing with your mouth closed—this is the behavior that civilized Western society expects. These manners don't come naturally. They must be learned and practiced until, with time, they become habit.

If a portion of the behavior that we consider "polite" is arbitrary, it's still true that a good deal of it does spring from simple consideration for other people, like opening a door for someone who's carrying shopping bags, or offering to bring a drink from the kitchen for anyone else who wants one. For most of us, considerate behavior has to be learned, too. Left to themselves, many children (and many adults) are not in the habit of thinking about what would be helpful, kind, or convenient for the people around them.

What's more, the Baby Boom generation has an extra handicap when it comes to manners. Having come of age in an era that made a point of discarding old-fashioned behavior, we have some trouble deciding what constitutes politeness. Is it all right for children to call grown-ups by their first names? And do you really have to write thank-you notes? And why can't you put your elbows on the table during meals, anyway? (Sometimes the answer is simply, "Because that's the way it's done.")

That is why I wrote this book. Manners move with the times, and the etiquette books I grew up with often suggest behavior that I don't think is appropriate any longer. My children are pretty polite, but I have not taught them to stand up when an adult enters the room. We live in an informal neighborhood so there are many adults whom they call by their first names. I'm not crazy about it, but I'll certainly go along with accepted practice. I am not interested in raising children whose behavior seems quaint: I just want them to be pleasant to have around.

With that goal in mind, I haven't emphasized especially formal behavior in this book. I'm more concerned with getting children to use any fork at all than with coaching them on the proper use of the fish fork. There are a couple of boxes on specific foods that require specific treatment, but since artichokes don't appear on our menu all that often, I haven't concentrated on that kind of thing.

Standards vary for different ages, too. You probably can't count on a six-year-old to introduce friends to each other, or a four-year-old to answer the phone politely. But any child who talks can say "Please" and "Thank you." This book is broken down by age groups to help you decide what's appropriate behavior at which age. And, yes, there *are* general expectations about manners. A seven-year-old can't get away with the kind of shy nonresponsiveness that's forgiven in a preschooler, for instance.

The idea here is that by the time your child turns six, he should be familiar with the concepts outlined in Part I, "Basic Training." Notice that I do not say he should have mastered them. At no time are you going to feel that your job is done: Teaching manners is one of parenthood's many unending tasks. Familiarity means that when you say, "Honey, can you remember to hold the door open for Aunt Martha?" this will not be a startling and radical notion. Holding the door should be a much-discussed feat that has been successfully carried out on several occasions, but not necessarily without prompting.

The sections of this book are cumulative. In other words, the polite world (your parents and mine) will expect a child of six to nine to be acquiring the behaviors in Part II, "The Age of Reason." And to have acquired those in Part I. By the preteen years, ten to twelve, a child should be learning the manners suggested in Part III, "The Young Sophisticate," as well as exhibiting with some consistency the manners set out in the earlier sections of the book. Some kinds of courtesy, like table manners and phone manners, appear in each section of the book, because what we expect of children in these areas changes as they get older. Other sections are specific to certain ages: There's no need to worry about romantic behavior with a seven-year-old, for instance. (For easy reference,

I've listed the rules at the beginning of each section.) I don't go into manners for teenagers because I'm afraid if you haven't caught your kids before then, it's a little late to start. Part IV outlines some specific ways we can make it easier for our children to learn good manners.

You will not be able to make your child perfect. Ever since I began working on this book, my friends have bombarded me with impossible dilemmas. "What can I do about Simon, who interrupts all the time?" "Josie said in the loudest voice, 'Why don't you have any hair?' and I thought I would die." "Mark just won't talk to our adult friends when they come over." Having good manners doesn't mean you never embarrass anyone or hurt anyone's feelings. What I hope for from my children is that overall, their behavior expresses respect and consideration for the people around them, and familiarity with the conventions of Western table manners. William is never going to overflow with exuberant small talk, and I will probably be nagging Timothy about talking with his mouth full until he leaves home for college. But already, at eight and five, they shake hands when they meet people, hold doors for grown-ups, and clear their places after meals.

My great fear is that people are going to look at these lists of rules and say, "This woman is out of her mind. I could never get my kids to do all that." I know. I won't be able to either. Not *all* of it. There will be things that just don't take. I am still, in spite of all my efforts, quick to interrupt people. My husband, who is honestly a paragon of manhood, seldom remembers to use a napkin. Nobody gets it all right.

But your child *can* learn most of this stuff. You have years to work on it. I have tried to be realistic about children's development, not only by using my sons as guinea pigs, but also by talking with parents across the country. The standards I'm proposing were arrived at by an informal consensus. There is nothing excessive or outlandish in what I'm suggesting. The next section gives some general suggestions about how to teach good manners. You start gradually. You remind often. And honestly, before you know it, the compliments will start coming in. "Jason is such a nice boy."

"You know, Caitlin does such a good job of answering the phone." "When Toby got up and cleared his dinner plate I almost fell flat on the floor." Teach your child the manners described here and he'll be more popular and more pleasant to have around. That's a promise.

Teaching Manners

Every now and then I read an article about one of those seminars given by an etiquette expert at a hotel. Children dress in their best clothes and, over lunch, learn how to spoon soup away from themselves and handle a big linen napkin.

That's a valid approach to learning the most formal table manners, but for most children it's too little too late. By the time a child is old enough to sit through several courses of an elaborate hotel lunch, he or she should already be well schooled in the basics. And while it can be valuable to have an expert introduce you to the complexities of a formal meal, I don't think that corresponds to the realities of most kids' lives. It would be a lot more interesting to get those etiquette experts behind the wheel of a minivan with a full load of hungry nine-year-old soccer players, and see what emerged at the end of the trip.

Teaching manners is a long-term project. What's more, it's a project you need to keep at the front of your mind all the time. It doesn't need to loom large, but it's something you should be aware of, just as you're always aware of your child's safety.

In fact, teaching children habits of safety is a good analogy. The first step is **modeling** the right behavior. You wear your seat belt, store matches out of reach, look both ways when you cross the street. By the same token, you need to model good manners for your children. Treat them as courteously as you hope they'll treat you one day. Say "Please" and "Thank you," and "Excuse me" if you need to interrupt. Be very careful during meals to take small bites, chew with your mouth closed, keep your elbows off the table. (Soon enough your children will be delighted to turn into manners police anyway, and they'll be helping you to remember all these things.) Modeling the behavior your want your children to emulate is the single most powerful thing you can do to teach them anything.

The second step is **gradually introducing new habits**. Say your child is five. Maybe there's something that's been bothering you about her behavior, or maybe you notice a couple of things that she's already on the road to doing right. I'd select just three or four things to work on in different areas, because a barrage of new requirements is counterproductive. Say you'd like to get her to sit still for ten minutes at dinnertime, and you'd like her to stop closing the door in your face. She's already pretty good about "please" and "thank you," so you can praise her for doing that right.

First you let her know what behavior you'd like to see: "Honey, could you hold the door open for me so it doesn't slam shut right in my face? Oh, thank you." Next time you remind her ahead of time: "Don't forget about the door . . . Wonderful." Then you take it a step further: "Can you hold the door open for this lady? Good." Finally, when she can remember to do it herself about half the time, it's time to move on to a new skill.

This may sound awkward, but you'll get a sense for when your child is ready for something new. For a long time when my older son Willy was six, I had to nag him constantly to sit with his legs down, instead of with his knees hunched up against the table. And then one day, I realized I wasn't bugging him about his knees any more. So I started in on not waving his fork around. Now, although his knees occasionally pop up and he sometimes gestures with a forkload of ravioli, we're concentrating on not shoveling food into a full mouth. Meanwhile, his little brother, Timo, is still back at the stage where we're hoping he uses a fork most of the time. Next on the agenda for him: napkin in the lap.

Encouragement is an essential component of this method. Praise helps children know when they're doing something right. I use it on every child who crosses the threshold, and this is how it usually works. Timo's little friend Gwen comes into the kitchen and says, "I'm hungry. Could I please have a snack?" I say to her, "Gwen, when you ask so nicely I'm happy to give you a snack. What would you like?" And of course she responds, as politely as she knows how, "I'd like some apple juice and crackers, please." (It's worth sounding like Mr. Rogers to get the results you want.) Children flourish on praise and they will repeat the behavior that nets it for them.

Another important technique is **consistency**. Sometimes you will encounter resistance, and it's important to stand firm. Otherwise you risk conveying the message that polite behavior isn't really that important after all. I'm not saying that you have to be rigid, and of course you'll relax your standards when your children are ill or exhausted. But it will be hard for them to learn manners if they have to be polite on some days but not on others. Once you've introduced a new behavior you need to be prepared to stick with it, through initial interest, subsequent resistance, and ultimate forgetfulness.

The final step toward teaching manners is **prompting**. A stream of gentle, courteous reminders about what behavior you expect is essential. My reminders are often indistinguishable from nagging, I have to admit, but my intentions are good. Remember, a lot of what you're teaching doesn't come naturally. That's why coaching is necessary. A few whispered words before a child meets an adult can smooth over an awkward introduction, for instance. A little exasperated screeching doesn't seem to do any permanent harm, either. And as long as you're after kids to do their homework and put their dirty socks in the laundry basket and feed the birds and turn the TV off, you might as well require good manners as well. They are just as important a set of skills as keeping a room neat. What's more, they are skills that can be used to good effect in any number of situations, for the rest of your child's life.

PART I

Basic Training

Ages 3-5

Nobody expects a three-year-old to be polite. Actually, a three-year-old with good manners would be kind of alarming; you'd wonder what the parents had done to get this very small child to behave so uniformly well.

So why bother? Why even attempt something that looks impossible? Why start worrying about having your child sit at the table through dinner when you are mostly concerned about getting some nutrients into her? Why fret about her habit of shrieking in the car when you can barely get the seat belt around her without resorting to violence? Can't this all wait until things are calmer?

Yes, of course it can. But there are three pressing reasons for starting to teach manners when your children are preschoolers. One is that manners have to be taught sometime, and they'll be a lot easier if you start early and gradually build skills. The second is that children of this age are so eager to please that it's a great time to teach them anything. They want to get it right to make you happy. But the best reason for starting to teach manners to preschoolers is simply this: It's very pleasant to live with children who treat you with even rudimentary courtesy.

A child at eighteen months is a force of nature, and you can't do much to tame her. She *should* be this way; investigating the environment is her life work at the moment. But by the time a child is three, she's learning the boundaries. She's discovering what's acceptable and what isn't. She's beginning to get civilized. Or socialized, if you'd rather think of it that way. You want her to share with her friends and to use words instead of hitting and to help clean up her toys after a play date. It's only a step beyond that to add basic politeness, like table manners and saying "Please" and "Thank you."

And believe me, teaching manners to small children is completely worthwhile. Let's look at the sitting-still-at-the-table issue. If your child is accustomed to sitting and eating for ten, fifteen, maybe twenty minutes, this gives you time to sit and have some (possibly disjointed) conversation with the whole family. I wouldn't suggest that meals are truly social yet, but you can see them heading in that direction. And you don't have to keep wondering where Ned has taken that hot dog and whether you'll find it before it starts to smell. You don't have to keep coaxing Meghan back to the table to eat just one more bite of corn. When she gets up for good, you know that she's really done. By the time your child is four, family dinner can really be quite pleasant. Amazing!

Of course, you don't want to squelch your child's free development of skills and healthy habits. A friend of mine whose young sons are very polite says she's careful not to nag her three-year-old about chewing with his mouth shut because, she says, "I'm more concerned that he chew at all, and enjoy his food." You certainly don't want to make a child timid or self-conscious by issuing too many directives.

What's more, there are certain niceties of behavior that preschoolers *can't* be taught. Most of them don't have the manual dexterity or strength to cut their own meat, for instance. Many youngsters are very shy with new grown-ups. Certainly you can't expect the average preschooler to handle the phone with aplomb.

So I don't address these concerns in this section of the book. There is, however, a lot of information about table manners. As I mentioned in the introduction, table manners are some of our most arbitrary customs. In fact, based as they are on medieval European courtesy, the very point of many of them is precisely their difficulty to master. It's hard to convey a fork loaded with food from a plate to the mouth. It would be much easier (and, to the average four-year-old, more sensible) to get a firm grasp on that hunk of potato with the fingers. But in the Middle Ages, it was precisely those hard-to-master skills that distinguished the upper crust from the peasants. So we're stuck with them. These skills are a lot for a small child to learn, but remember, you're not attacking them all at once. Nor do you expect perfection—ever.

In fact, looking over the subjects intended for this section, I realize that in many areas I don't really expect my preschooler to have *mastered* the behavior suggested. What I do want is for him to recognize and respond to my reminders. For instance, it is undeniably polite to accompany your guests to the door when they leave your house. This is true whether they are four or forty. Sometimes Timothy gets caught up in the leave-taking process and stands waving at the door as if his friends were about to cross Kansas in a covered wagon. Sometimes he can't be bothered to lift his head from the Legos to say good-bye. But since I have coached him on this and let him know that a cordial farewell is expected, he will usually (if grudgingly) comply.

And that's good enough for me.

• GENERATION GAP •

I tend to get very nervous and picky about my children's manners when we're around people of my parents' generation. These, after all, were the people who taught us always to call them Mr. and Mrs., or even Sir and Ma'am. They insisted that we clean our plates, and may even have forced us to wear little white gloves like Minnie Mouse's.

So what can these people possibly think about our children? And, by extension, about our skills as parents?

Who cares? Repeat after me: Who cares?

The sensible ones will withhold judgment and realize that your children are nice even if they don't know how to use a finger bowl. The rigid ones have written you off from the moment you appeared with your son in sweat pants instead of gray flannel shorts, and with your daughter wearing, heaven help us all, bright pink leggings (instead of a nice neat navy blue jumper). You can't please 'em, so don't worry about 'em.

Meeting Adults

One of the most important things we can teach our children is how to meet new people with comfort and ease. It's a part of life that makes everyone nervous. As adults we have to do it and pretend we don't mind, but I know I always feel awkward. And that's after forty years of experience.

One way to help children with this hurdle is to make sure they know exactly what they're supposed to do when they meet people. Smile? Wave? Speak? Ignore the whole thing? Social unease often looks like sulkiness from the outside, and those cast-down eyes, inaudible voice, and shuffling feet that drive you nuts may be a response to plain old ignorance of what's expected. Your kids will be much more comfortable if you teach them a routine for introductions.

You have to wait until they're ready, of course. A child's awkwardness may be based on more than just lack of information. It could be what our parents called "a stage" ("a developmental issue" in the lingo of the nineties). Many preschoolers are not comfortable enough with strangers to shake hands and say hello with aplomb. And that's fine: Most people are understanding of a four-year-old child who burrows his head into your leg and refuses to utter a word. Prompting and coaxing, or making an excuse like "Toby's feeling shy today" only draws attention to poor old Toby, who wishes people would stop looking at him. If your preschooler is shy with new people, talk right over him (maybe with a reassuring hand on his shoulders). Often, once a child senses that nobody's paying any attention to him, he'll emerge from his shelter behind Mom to check out a new person and possibly even offer a greeting.

Children acquire social ease at different ages, depending on their temperaments. Sometimes an outgoing second child can mimic an elder sibling's behavior, working a room like an old politician at an age when the elder was still mute. Good-natured people tend to be tolerant of shyness, but by the time your child finishes kindergarten, she should be able to greet an adult this way:

Say "Hello."

Or "Hi." The point is that your child should acknowledge people's presence vocally. And even if your kid's incredibly shy, if she fails to say "Hello," it looks as if he's ignoring this person. It's all the more crucial if the grown-up has already said "Hello, Matthew." Your kid just has to answer.

It's especially nice if he can answer using this person's name. "Hi, Mr. Frankel." Or "Hi, Nicole." Your job here is to make sure the child knows what the name is. The etiquette books I grew up with are full of formulas dealing with who should be introduced to whom: Whose name gets said first indicates who is more important socially. I don't think most of us notice that anymore, at least not with kids around. All you need to say is, "Irene, this is my daughter Matilda. Matilda, this is Ms. Maxwell." And then Matilda's line is, "Hello, Ms. Maxwell." If you keep repeating the formula, your child will eventually get it right. If you want to go one step further, you can add a little information to identify this strange grown-up, like "Mrs. Taylor is a friend of your Aunt Sophie's" or "Stephen teaches at Elmwood School."

Corny as it seems, this is a situation that you can practice ahead of time. A preschooler fortunately doesn't know what corny is, and would be perfectly happy to act out meeting people over and over again, especially if you were willing to put on a funny hat or use weird names to liven things up.

Look people in the eye.

A great trick that I learned from etiquette expert Marjabelle Young Stewart is to instruct your child to notice someone's eye color when they meet. This gives them something mundane to think about at an awkward moment, and the result is the desired open, frank gaze. Children who like statistics can keep tallies of brown versus blue eyes, eyeglasses, bushy eyebrows, and so on.

Shake hands.

It's never too early to start. Even though your preschooler can't tell left from right, there's something extremely appealing about a small pink paw stuck out as a courteous gesture. It used to be that little girls were taught to curtsy instead of shaking hands, but those days are long gone. There are still, in very formal circles, rules about who is supposed to offer his hand first (the social superior, if you can figure out who that is) but that's much too complicated a concept for parents to bother with.

These three rules aren't much to learn, and it's often possible to prompt your child in a whisper before she actually has to face up to a strange adult. And believe me, there are few things your child can do that will make a better initial impression than shaking hands, looking someone in the eye, and saying "Hello."

Table Manners

The Basic Rules:

Stay seated • Sitting means sitting • Don't eat before everyone else does • Chew with your mouth closed • Don't talk with food in your mouth • Don't eat with your fingers • Use the correct utensil • Don't wave utensils around • No playing with food • No shoveling food • Eat only off your own plate • Don't say the food is yucky. • Use your napkin, not your shirt • Elbows off the table. • Keep your free hand in your lap • No singing at the table • Ask to be excused • Clear your place

My husband and I used to refer to family dinner as "Dining Hell." When our younger son first graduated from the high chair, he sat directly across from me at the table and I simply couldn't bear the combination of excessive demands and mess, so I switched places to get away from him. I'm happy to say that the situation has improved a great deal since then, but dinner with the boys is still a sight that would appall anyone with a taste for decorum. And the floor under the table needs cleaning after every single meal or snack, which doesn't mean it gets it.

We do have our standards; however. It is possible and desirable to insist on certain behavior, which will lay the groundwork for more attractive dining experiences down the road. This is the longest section in Part I, and you obviously can't introduce all these concepts at once. The most basic ones—staying at the table and using utensils—are crucial to pleasant meals, and it's worth spending several months on these issues. You can add the refinements, like keeping elbows off the table, once the fundamentals are fairly consistently in place.

Stay seated.

Small children need to understand that meals are eaten sitting down at a table. This is easier to put across (and your vacuuming will be reduced) if you forbid eating anywhere else. That means no eating on the sofa while watching TV, and it also means that *you* can't eat crackers in bed when your children are watching.

The other half of this principle involves keeping children at the table. Once they sit down to eat, they stay there until they're done, and they can't come back. No wandering away to dump out the Tinker Toys and returning for a few more grapes. This is *really important.* If your family meals currently involve children milling around the table chewing, you won't believe how restful it is to have everybody sitting in one place for a few minutes. (It could be as few as ten. Preschoolers' appetites are inconsistent and there's no point in forcing them to sit still after they've finished eating.)

The way to make this rule stick is simple, though it may seem harsh. When a child leaves the table, warn him that he can't come back later for more. Be sure to mention dessert. Then, if he gets up anyway, remove the plate. And don't give it back. It's worth suffering through quite a few tantrums to make this lesson stick, and only the stubbornest child will test you that far. Most of them will catch on after one or two efforts. And if they complain about hunger later in the day or evening, point out the folly of leaving the table before you're really done with the meal. Both of my children have gone through phases of doing this, and it's not easy to look down on a little person in bed who's saying in a plaintive voice, "I'm hungry." But they did learn very quickly that this pitiful approach didn't work at all. The kitchen is closed after dinner. Period.

If this technique isn't your style, or if you don't think you're going to be able to stand firm, don't even try it. You don't want to give mixed messages by telling your child that he has to stay seated at the table to eat, and then giving him more food when he comes back weeping. An alternative method is simply to remove the chair of a child who keeps leaving the table. It's less effective, because the novelty of eating standing up is attractive at first. But at least the undesirable behavior of leaving the table does provoke a response. And eating standing up isn't fun for long.

Sitting means sitting.

Not kneeling or perching or slouching. I wouldn't insist on a really small child sitting properly, but once she's tall enough to do without a booster seat, she should sit on her bottom with her feet straight in front of her. No knees up, no legs crossed, no chins in plates. I sometimes remind the boys that they aren't basset hounds, eating off the floor. Also rocking the chair—currently irresistible to both of my sons—is a no-no.

Don't eat before everyone else does.

This is more of an ideal than a rule. If your schedule means that your very young children are ravenous when they get to the table, you can't ask them to wait until everyone is served. By the time a child is four or five, though, you can institute some kind of official beginning to the meal.

One way this might work is to have fruit or raw vegetables on the table as you're getting ready to serve, and they can be eaten before everyone's seated. (This gives them a bit of forbidden-fruit glamour, which vegetables can always use.) Then, when even the cook is sitting in front of her plate, someone gives the "all clear" signal. Some families say a blessing or a grace. My mother used to just say, "You may start." You could even teach your children to watch Mom, and when she lifts her fork, they can too. After all, this is how it's done in polite society. And the great thing about everyone starting dinner at once is that the children aren't finished and clamoring for dessert before you've swallowed your first bite of broccoli.

Chew with your mouth closed.

Some cultures interpret slurping and smacking as signs of gusto, and when you watch babies eat, this seems reasonable. But Western manners insist that food vanish silently into the mouth, to be seen and heard no more. Chewing noiselessly may not come naturally but it doesn't require any special coordination from your child: just lots of reminders from you.

Don't talk with food in your mouth.

Many adults are guilty of this practice, too. Probably most of us. But adults can manage to shovel a small portion of food off to the side of their mouths and still speak somewhat clearly. This is too hard for kids. When they try to talk through a mouthful of graham cracker, you say pleasantly, "Chew and swallow, honey, I can't understand what you're saying with food in your mouth." In their eagerness to communicate, they'll cooperate. This is a procedure you can expect to repeat about a million times in the next fifteen years. Believe it or not, though, your children will eventually pick up the habit. Our older son has reached the point where he will chew and swallow before answering a question—three times out of five, anyway.

Don't eat with your fingers.

You will have to be the judge of when to apply this rule. Some foods are simply devilish for a small child to manage with utensils, and some parents are so happy to see their children eating that they don't want to complicate the experience. By around the age of four, though, the roster of finger foods should be shrinking. You may be able to sell your child on consistently using utensils by getting her a special "big girl" spoon and fork. Some children may also find eating easier if they have a pusher, which is a utensil shaped like a broad hoe that little ones can use to push food onto their forks. You can expect your child to use her hands for assistance for quite some time—picking up a piece of chicken to jam it securely onto her fork, for instance. It's hard to eat with these ridiculous tools we call cutlery, and learning how will take a lot of practice and many reminders from you.

Use the correct utensil.

Spoons are generally easier than forks, but somewhere along the line, at least by the age of six, children need to learn how to use forks for most foods. You can help this transition along by neglecting to set a spoon at your child's place and serving foods that are easier to manage with a fork. In other words, steer clear of the peas for a little while.

Don't wave utensils around.

This might not occur to you until you see your six-year-old gesturing with a forkload of mashed potatoes. Utensils should, ideally, go from plate to mouth and back to plate. They can be rested on the plate for a little pause (not likely if a child's in charge). But they should not describe arcs in the air. The reminder we end up using is "Don't wave your fork around," but when I was a child my mother got some mileage out of military-style "square meals." She told us that at West Point, cadets were supposed to make squares in the air with their forks: Lift them straight up from the plate, move horizontally to the mouth, lower to table level, and move across to the plate. I have no idea if this is really part of military training, but it got her point across. None of us has ever stabbed anyone in the eye with a fork.

No playing with food.

The great thing about food from a kid's point of view is that you can make it into other things. A carrot stick is a cigarette or a gun. A slice of cheese is a mustache. Spaghetti is a bird's nest, and you can bite pieces of pear into magnificent false teeth. As a parent, you can't completely halt this—and you wouldn't really want to— but a very little bit of it goes a long way, especially when you're a guest at someone else's table. If certain foods always spark imaginary play, you can ban them for a few days, making sure your kids know why. (Maybe put a big sign on the refrigerator door. An apple, for instance, crossed out.) You want to communicate the idea that you're serious about this, without coming across as a prison warden.

No shoveling food.

By shoveling I mean the style of eating where a bite goes in, is partially chewed, and the mouth is opened for another bite before the first bite is swallowed. This is gross. It is also, for some children, the natural way to eat. But they should chew and swallow each bite completely before taking in the next. Or before taking a swig of milk. Again, reminders are necessary. But it's especially important to establish good habits in this regard before children reach the point where they enjoy nothing so much as cramming their mouths full to bursting.

Eat only off your own plate.

There's something appealing on a primal level about sharing food with a small child, and few parents will stop a two-year-old from plucking a green bean or a bite of chicken off the adult's plate. This behavior is much less forgivable, though, in an older child, and a sibling will resent it deeply. Simply keeping plates out of reach of a grabber will help.

Don't say the food is yucky.

No matter what your policy is on tasting or eating or leaving food on the plate, no food should be disparaged. You can't stop children from finding okra disgusting, but you can cut short a detailed tirade on exactly how repulsive it is. A calm take-it-or-leave-it attitude, while almost impossible to maintain, is the best way to silence the symphony of disgust. (See page 133, "Yucky Food")

Use your napkin, not your shirt.

Little kids are messy eaters so they need to wipe their mouths and hands a lot. The easiest way for them to do this is to draw an arm clad in a long-sleeved shirt across their mouths, and to wipe their sticky fingers on their tummies. The correct way, though, is to use a napkin. The napkin belongs in the lap, where it is spread out to catch spills. Between bites, or at an adult's command, it is lifted to wipe the mouth, then replaced in the lap. Since children don't care that their mouths are smeared with food, or that their shirts are spattered with gravy, use of the napkin does not come naturally. This means constant reminders. Like after every bite: "Susan, wipe your mouth with your napkin." It's worth noting that cloth napkins are easier than flimsy paper ones to handle, and if you get patterned, permanent press ones, you won't have to wash them all that often, either. (Just don't tell Grandma.)

Elbows off the table.

This rule guarantees that nobody encroaches on anyone else's personal space, and also that nobody props a head on a hand and flops over the plate like a plant in need of water. No preschooler needs to know the rationale, though. Just teach them the rhyme I learned from a friend's five-year-old: "Mabel, Mabel, if you're able, Keep your elbows off the table."

Keep your free hand in your lap.

I know, I know, how many grown-ups follow this rule? But think of all the mischief those hands can get into: fiddling with salt shakers, crumbling pieces of bread, pulling at the fringe on a place mat. Wouldn't you rather have that idle hand safely below the table, holding the napkin in place? As long as dinner is going to be punctuated with advice, you might as well add this piece.

No singing at the table.

The ideal mealtime entertainment is pleasant general conversation. If someone is performing, conversation is impossible. What's more, anyone who's singing can't eat. So if your four-year-old spends ten minutes doing Little Richard's version of "The Eensy Weensy Spider," she's preventing you from chatting with your spouse (because you, of course, are too polite to talk while she's singing), and she's falling behind in the race for dessert. A flat ban on music at meals is pretty easy to institute and maintain. If it seems too harsh, try building a song into the meal ritual, as a kind of grace beforehand or even entertainment afterward. One of the small difficulties of family dinner is that kids are always done before the grown-ups. Our younger son usually wolfs down his food and either tries to pry himself into somebody's lap or settles under the table, where he always gets kicked. We have sometimes short-circuited a burst of song during the meal or kept him busy afterward by suggesting he sing for us as soon as he's done eating. That buys us peace for at least four more minutes. On the other hand, if your children don't burst into song a lot, don't even mention this. No point in putting ideas into their heads.

Ask to be excused.

Children should always ask to leave the table. "May I please be excused?" is a pretty simple formula, or they could say, "May I get down from the table?" Sometimes you'll hear nothing but a muttered string of syllables flung at you on the way back to the dollhouse. Sometimes you'll have to bring a child gently back to the table and reseat him, saying, "You need to ask to be excused." And sometimes you'll meet resistance, but you need to keep plugging away. This little ritual is important because it signals to everyone a distinct closure to the meal. This is the point after which there is no coming back to the table for more food.

Clear your place.

If your children eat off fairly light unbreakable plates, and if the kitchen counter isn't too far away from the table where you eat most meals, and if there are no tricky swing doors or steps in between, they can and should take their plates and cutlery and cups off the table and put them next to the sink. I wouldn't have thought this was possible until I saw Timo's preschool classmates at the end of lunch one day, all carefully clearing their plates and scraping them into the garbage. None of them was yet four. I figured if he could do it at school, he could do it at home, and he does, with minimal breaking or spilling involved. If you present this as a privilege—"Now you're old enough to clear your place"—and load on the praise when it's done, it shouldn't be hard to teach.

You may be horrified at the length of this section, but all of these behaviors really are within the grasp of preschoolers, and you don't have to teach them all at once. What's more, you're bound to be thrilled by how much other adults appreciate good table manners in children. Pretty soon, the compliments will be rolling in, and you'll realize that you're really doing your children a big favor by teaching them how to eat politely.

• TOUCH AND TAKE •

About a year ago we were at a party where plates of raw vegetables sat on tables at our four-year-old's eye level. There was a big crowd, so I lost sight of him for a while. But I could tell where he'd been when I reached for a piece of zucchini and discovered that it bore a crescent of small tooth marks. Clearly he hadn't grasped the "touch and take" principle.

Assimilating this one depends on temperament. A thoughtful, careful child of five will probably survey a plate of crackers carefully before choosing the one that looks best to him. It's going against nature, though, to ask most younger children to consider before touching food. You need to be at their side, ready to intercept the grab ("Is that the one you really want? Wouldn't you rather have one without sesame seeds?"). Or be prepared to pocket the evidence of their tasting experiments.

Manners of Speech

The Basic Rules:

Use "inside voices" • No interrupting • Say "Excuse me" if you must interrupt • Say "Excuse me" when you burp • No chanting • No name-calling • Say "Please" and "Thank you" • Bathroom words stay in the bathroom

---

"Use words," you keep urging as your toddler howls. "Use words." After all, words are what distinguish us from animals. But *how* words are used matters, too.

Children will absorb many of the subtleties of speech from the adults around them. If you listen attentively to them without interrupting, and ask questions to draw further information from them, they will understand that this is how conversation works. But modeling good conversational skills isn't quite enough. Preschoolers will need to have the following principles spelled out—again and again and again.

Use "inside voices."

Kids have no idea how loud they are, and if they knew they wouldn't care. So you have to remind them that the kind of volume that works on the playground is a little much in the living room, where they should use an "inside voice." I haven't yet met a child younger than ten who will lower her voice without being reminded. I honestly don't think they can hear themselves. So *you* need to be able to bring the volume down time and again, gently, without getting annoyed. If your child is inclined to be boisterous you might even want to invent a secret signal (a tug on the ear, maybe) to use in company.

Introducing a note of fantasy can also calm things down. Timo's preschool teacher used to suggest that the children pretend to be mice or burglars whenever she really needed them to pipe down. It worked like a dream.

No interrupting.

We take turns when we're talking. This is a pretty complicated skill to master because you have to interpret cues, like a falling inflection at the end of a sentence, that let you know the speaker's finished. (This is why phone conversations with preschoolers are so often punctuated by long pauses.)

It's also hard for small fry to hold onto their thoughts until their turn arrives. So you have to remind your preschooler about not interrupting (and your older children, too). It's more a principle you're introducing than an actual achievable goal. Feel free to stop a child who has interrupted and say, "Your sister was talking, honey. Let her finish, then you can talk." Be sure to keep your own voice quiet or you'll get into the escalating volume spiral.

Say "Excuse Me" if you must interrupt.

Sometimes kids just have to interrupt, especially if their mom hasn't noticed that the bus is coming or the bathtub is overflowing. Make this explicit: Point out to your child that sometimes people do have to interrupt and that this is the polite way to do it. The best way to reinforce this habit is to stop whatever you're saying and pay complete attention to the child who politely breaks into your conversation.

Say "Excuse me" when you burp.

After the gales of giggles have died down, that is. Eventually, maybe when your child is nineteen, he'll excuse himself automatically after a burp or a sneeze and nobody will laugh. Until then, you'll have to prompt him: "What do you say?"

No chanting.

I was astonished when Willy came home from preschool saying, "Nah-nah-nah boo-boo, you can't catch me" in *that* tone of voice. I guess I thought something might have replaced that nyah-nyah form of derision in the thirty-odd years since I was a kid, but apparently this is a permanent feature of childhood. And kids are as sensitive to it as they ever were. One of Willy's teachers called this "chanting" and it's a good term for something that's otherwise a little hard to explain. You can't say to a preschooler, "Don't use that tone of voice" because he won't understand. But if you say, "No chanting, please, it hurts people's feelings," and demonstrate what you mean, you've made yourself clear.

No name-calling.

Calling people names hurts their feelings, too. This is really a discipline issue, on a par with "no hitting" and "no throwing sand," but I put it here so nobody thinks I'm overlooking it.

Say "Please" and "Thank you."

Anyone who can say those words, or something approximating them, should. By the time your child is four she should, at least sometimes, thank you without prompting. Or say, "Mom, could you please braid my hair?" without thinking. You can expect to remind kids about this many thousands of times between now and adolescence. It's at least as effective to say, from time to time, "I really appreciate it when you ask for things so nicely."

Bathroom words stay in the bathroom.

A fascination with bathroom talk is common in preschoolers, who enjoy the adult reaction to these words. You can spoil some of their fun by failing to react, and you can also send them off to the bathroom to discuss bodily functions until they get bored. Which will be quickly.

• F O R B I D D E N   W O R D S •

Bathroom talk aside, we all have words that we prefer not to hear from our children. Some kids will test you by seeing what happens when they use X-rated vocabulary, and some burst into gales of giggles at anything suggesting anatomical functions. They're experimenting with the power of language and that's appropriate. But you know what? They don't have to do it around you. You can ban certain words from your hearing. They don't all have to be dirty words, either.

We struck a deal with my older son when he was five. I didn't like to hear him say "hate," "stupid," or "bored." He gave this some thought, and said, "Well, I don't like certain words either." That seemed fair enough. The words he disliked were "handsome," "cute," and "lovely." The deal was that if I used one of his forbidden words, he could say one of mine, and vice versa. If I told him he looked handsome (a horrific concept to him, apparently), he could look me in the eye and say, "stupid." Mind you, he wasn't *calling* me stupid, just uttering the word. And if he said "I'm bored," I could say "cute."

It's worked. I may have to expand the horizons soon to include "butt" and "dumb," but it's a good-natured arrangement that benefits both of us. Little does he know that I call him handsome when he's asleep.

• COMPLIMENTS •

My mother always taught me that if you like something about somebody, you should tell them. If you think their hair looks pretty or they have a nifty new car or you like the chili they brought to the potluck supper, you let that person know. And Mom was right. Think how great you felt the last time somebody said something nice to you.

Some people are more observant than others, and a happy, outgoing child may have an innate talent for flattery. Last fall when I picked Timothy up from preschool I was wearing a brooch to hold my sweater closed since the button was missing. He looked at it, fingered it, and said, "I like your beautiful pin, Mommy." I can imagine this direct approach being extremely effective with women of all ages in years to come.

But more reserved children can be taught to praise too. The first step is to praise them, not necessarily lavishly but with sincerity. Then point out how much people appreciate compliments. Remind your daughter how wonderful it made you feel when she said she liked the way you'd built the snowman, cut her sandwich, curled your hair. If she ever praises anyone to you ("I like the way Mrs. Toledo sings") say, "You should let her know. People always love to be told things like that." Of course it takes some nerve to do this, but people really do appreciate compliments so much that they react strongly and favorably. The obvious pleasure compliments give may encourage a shy child.

Responding to a compliment is much simpler. You say "Thank you." This is easy to convey to a child, since it's a rote response and always appropriate. "You have such good manners." "Thank you." Big smile. Enough said.

Play Dates

The Basic Rules:

Host greets guests • Guests pick what to do first •
Guests go along with host's wishes • Don't eat or
drink anything without sharing • Obey house rules
• Take your guest to the door to say good-bye •
Thank your host and the grown-up in charge when
you leave

I will never forget what a relief it was the first time I took my older son to play with a little friend, watched them dive into the Duplo blocks, said good-bye, and left. It was like seeing land on the horizon after years at sea: There was a time coming when my child would be more interested in other children—*any* other children—than he was in me. But of course, if I wanted to be sure he was invited frequently for play dates, he would have to be a reliably good guest.

Think about this for a moment. Aren't there some children you're more reluctant to have in your house than others? The ones who hog the new toys, grab cookies, and use the sofa as a trampoline are certainly the ones I don't ask over too often, and I hope my kids don't behave like that at other people's houses. There's a trick here, though. Since I'm not around to remind them to behave pleasantly, I've had to make sure that the boys have a pretty good grasp of play-date courtesy before I turn them loose on their buddies and *their* parents.

The only way I've come up with to accomplish this goal is to keep half an ear out for the dynamics of their at-home play dates, and to make sure that they're cooperating. And of course at drop-off and pick-up time I'm around to insist that they come up with the required "Hello," "Good-bye," and "Thank you." To wit:

Host greets guests.

Anyone, adult or child, feels more welcome if you come to the door and say hello. If you have to excavate your child from under the bed to extract a welcome, her guest may have second thoughts. This idea isn't easy to sell to a three-year-old, but when you think how she races to the door when her very best friend comes over, you can see how nice that is. More reserved children—or those who are deeply occupied building a castle out of blocks—may need to be reminded that, not ten minutes ago, they were bugging you about when Milo was coming and now here Milo is and they need to say hello to him.

Guests pick what to do first.

With very young children, of course, you can't enforce this idea. Any conflict will be better resolved by compromise or distraction, or by what one four-year-old friend calls "playing side by side." But you can introduce the notion of honoring a guest's wishes. And I think some five-year-olds are able to play checkers *first* to make a guest happy and *then* get the Barbies out. In that case, though, you must make sure that the host child does get some time doing her activity of choice, or she'll feel justifiably cheated.

Guests go along with the host's wishes.

If you can establish a pattern of taking turns that your children are secure with, they're more likely to be patient about their desires when they're guests. I know these two points are very difficult, and we have tears aplenty accompanying complaints that "Michael wants to play cowboys but I want to have a parade." I don't honestly expect compliance on these two principles, but I think it's really important to introduce them and keep them before my children. I sometimes have to intervene to help them work out a compromise, but I let them go as far as they can with the negotiating, and they get better and better at it.

Don't eat or drink anything without sharing.

Grown ups are in charge of doling out food and drink to pre-schoolers, so this is a good time to teach the sharing lesson. If Evan has been hoarding his Halloween candy and wants to polish off the candy corn, point out that he has to offer some to Henry, or else save it for later. Maybe there are only three ginger snaps left and both Keisha and Laura want them. Then each girl gets one and a half cookies. We've been through this little ritual so often (willingly or unwillingly) that the boys have accepted it and offer treats to their guests with fairly good grace.

Obey house rules.

If the Larkins take their shoes off when they step in the door, so do their guests. If they put one toy away before getting another out, so do their playmates. And so on. Most small children will readily obey unfamiliar adults, so when Mrs. Larkin says, "You need to eat that popsicle outside," Janie will comply. It is worth mentioning this idea, though, especially if your child sometimes plays with people whose style is very different from yours. Three-year-olds are sophisticated enough to understand that things are done differently in different places.

Take your guest to the door to say good-bye.

Out of sight, out of mind is the usual attitude with children. By the time the guest is in the hall putting on her jacket, her hostess is already rearranging the scarves in the dress-up box. The play date is over and she's moved on to something else. Hanging around in the hall saying good-bye isn't interesting. But it's polite and it makes guests feel cherished, so children should do it. Even if they have to be dragged by their parents.

Thank your host and the grown-up in charge when you leave.

This is for the guest, of course. And like the courtesy mentioned above, it probably won't happen without parental prompting. Usually when my children hear me saying, "Thanks for having Timo (or Willy) over," they'll chime in. It's a small point, but since it's the last impression your child makes on his pal's mom or baby-sitter, it has a lot of impact.

You hope, of course, that as a guest your child will do all those things you bug her about at home: eat neatly, say please and thank you, keep her voice to a conversational level. I wouldn't stress these things too much, though. I'm a staunch advocate of coaching kids for unusual occasions like lunch at a restaurant with Grandma. But I don't think it's a good idea to say to a child, as you drop him off for a play date, "Be sure to say please and thank you to Tina's mom." That adds a level of performance anxiety to the whole occasion (not to mention what it will do to a kid for whom separation is an issue). When all's said and done, play dates are about having fun.

• "RUDE" AND "POLITE" •

You can't teach a child good manners without that child's cooperation, so the first step is to make the goal—being polite—seem attractive. The easiest way to do this (and I admit it's simplistic) is to tell your child that polite behavior makes people feel good. And if they feel good, they'll like you.

You can illustrate this with examples. "How does it make you feel when Toni says she likes your picture? And you like Toni when she does that, don't you? That's polite." Use the term when you reinforce your child's behavior, too. If, by a miracle, she says, "Can you please tie my shoe?" then you say something like, "You're so polite! Of course I'll tie your shoe." And then of course when you finish the double knot, she'll say, "Thank you." And you'll say, "You're welcome," and you'll both be pleased with yourselves and each other.

Rude behavior also needs to be defined and identified. It's when somebody does something that makes you feel bad. Calling names is rude, ignoring somebody is rude, making faces is rude. Picking up an extension phone when somebody is on the line is rude. Sometimes children are rude out of emotional distress: When a child calls you names in a tantrum, what you really need to address is the tantrum, not the name-calling. But there are many times when they are just behaving naturally and you need to inform them gently that, for instance, pointing at that man on crutches is rude because it might hurt his feelings. (Never tell a child, though, that a friend's behavior is rude, since this presents a test of loyalty. Who does he like better, his mom or his rude friend? You don't want to know.)

Once you've defined your terms in a way that a preschooler grasps, you make it clear that polite behavior is appreciated while rude behavior is not. Preschoolers are so eager to please that they will usually try, if they aren't too busy or too annoyed with you, to be polite. The rest of your job is simply to help them know what's polite in what situation.

• MAKING MANNERS A TEAM EFFORT •

I've directed this book to parents, because I assume that it's mostly the parents of a child who will be concerned enough about his manners to teach courtesy in a systematic way. But many parents, of course, share child-rearing with former spouses or caregivers or in-laws or day care staff. So how can you get everybody on the same wavelength about the importance of teaching polite behavior?

I think you do it gradually. First, you set an example by insisting on courteous behavior from your child. When his grandmother gives your son a cookie, you prompt him to say "Thank you." When you pick your daughter up from day care, you whisper to her, "Did you say good-bye to Mrs. Starr?"

Second, you make your mission explicit. You say to your caregiver, "I think we need to work a little bit on Scotty's manners. It's driving me nuts the way he never says 'Please' or 'Thank you.' " Or you ask, at the day care center, "Does Tiana stay sitting down during lunch? We've been working on that at home, but she keeps getting up, and I wondered if you were having better luck than we are." Without giving orders, you are just letting people know that your child's level of courtesy is important to you.

And finally, you can solicit help as you're concentrating on particular areas of manners. You can say, as you leave your children with your mother for an evening, "By the way, we're working on learning how to cut meat the right way. How did you teach us that?" Or announce on Monday morning to the caregiver, "This weekend Arthur decided he was old enough to clear his plate after his meal, isn't that great?"

These suggestions may sound stilted or corny, but you'll find more natural ways to share your goals with the people who are helping rear your children. You keep them up to date on discipline and development in other areas: That's a natural process and part of the give and take of delegating child-rearing. Just add manners into the mix, along with all those other crucial skills your children are mastering.

Telephone Manners

The Basic Rules:

Say who you are • Say "May I please speak to . . ."
• Speak slowly • Talk in a normal tone of voice •
Keep the call short • Social plans made on the phone
must be approved by a parent • Say "Good-bye"
when you're finished • Don't listen to other people's
calls on an extension • Don't press the buttons when
someone is talking on the phone • Don't yell into an
extension when someone is on another phone

Our phone rang at ten minutes after seven on a recent Saturday morning. I rushed dripping out of the bathroom to answer it, sure that only an emergency would prompt someone to call us at that hour on a weekend. I was a little taken aback to hear the peremptory tones of a five-year-old coming down the wire. "I want to talk to Timo," she announced. I was less than charmed. I was also surprised that this child's mother, whom I respect, allowed her daughter to make this dawn phone call. Of course, the girl is precocious and perfectly capable of memorizing a seven-digit telephone number, so for all I know, her mom was still in the shower herself. Or asleep, like Timo.

You forget, until you get an inappropriate call like this one, that the telephone projects you into somebody else's life. Adult phone use is governed by an elaborate system of courtesy that's all the more important because we're dealing only with voices here. When we talk to people face-to-face we get a lot of information from their expression and body language. The phone takes those away, so we never see the sweet smile that might have reconciled us to a preschooler's abruptness.

We have to teach kids this system so they can use the phone politely. Instinct isn't going to help them much, as anybody knows who has seen a three-year-old nod her head in response to a question from Granny calling long distance. What's more, in most households, the telephone is grown-up territory and the primary link to bosses, clients, elderly relatives, and childless friends, as well as to those who have their own children. Many adults are not amused by the heavy-breathing panic or garbled greeting of a small child at the other end of the wire. Yes, of course preschoolers can talk on the phone. But they need a parent standing by. Grown-ups should dial the phone, because children aren't familiar with the keypad so they have to hunt and peck. Sometimes the circuits aren't quite patient enough to handle long gaps between numbers. And small children have to be told what we take for granted—what all those weird beeps and buzzes mean. They don't know, unless you tell them, when you're actually supposed to start talking. If you are standing at your child's elbow, you can prompt her in a whisper. Most kids will be glad of a little coaching, because using the phone is unnerving at first.

These guidelines, by the way, are geared for children making calls under adult supervision. I don't think preschoolers should answer the telephone. Most calls in the average household will be for adults or for older siblings, whose callers may not be patient with a small child. If, however, you insist on putting your unbelievably mature four-year-old in charge of incoming calls, see Part II for suggested behavior.

Say who you are.

"Hello, this is Melanie" should be the first line out of your little caller's mouth. The person on the other end will be more patient with Melanie than he would with an unidentified childish caller.

Say "May I please speak to. . . ."

The "please" is especially important. Little kids often sound curt or bossy on the phone. If they forget to say please, the grown-up on the other end feels as if she's being ordered around by a person half her size. This does not create warm feelings.

Speak slowly.

Nervous people, no matter how old, tend to talk fast. When you combine this tendency with the undeveloped speech of a pre-schooler, you've got incomprehensible gabble. Remind your child to slow down.

Talk in a normal tone of voice.

Some kids have louder voices than others. These are also the kids who tend to get louder when they're anxious, so they may need to be reminded to pipe down. On the other hand, there are the whisperers, who just get quieter and quieter until they're inaudible. Sometimes they clam up entirely, so you need to be ready to take over for them.

Keep the call short.

Remember, even if your child had a concrete purpose in calling his buddy Scooter, it probably wasn't complicated. ("Guess what, I got a red Power Ranger sweatshirt!") No need to prolong things.

Social plans made on the phone must be approved by a parent.

This winter a child was pleading with me to bring my son over to his house to play. It was sleeting, and the ground was covered with a thin skim of ice. I said I was a mean mommy, but I wasn't going outside. "My mom will come and get him!" this boy offered. There was a noise of the phone changing hands. The mom came on the phone and apologetically reneged on her son's offer. I was completely sympathetic. Kids not only have no sense of time, they also don't value physical comfort. This makes them poor planners.

Say "Good-bye" when you're finished.

Hanging up on somebody without warning is one of the most powerfully rude techniques available to grown-ups. Small children shouldn't use it unwittingly.

There are a few additional rules about the phone that young children need to learn, even if they aren't ready to launch into major chatting.

Don't listen to other people's calls on an extension.

When a child discovers that you can pick up the kitchen phone and hear Dad's conversation from the bedroom, that's interesting. Kind of magical. It won't occur to most preschoolers that listening to adult conversations is rude and distracting to the adults talking. This should be explained.

Don't press the buttons when someone is talking on the phone.

A child won't know, until you tell her, that when you press that little button you disconnect the call.

Don't yell into an extension when someone is on another phone.

This is so rude that if it happens more than once, it's time to cut the call short and embark on some serious disciplinary measures.

The telephone is going to become a bigger and bigger part of your child's life, and if you start early with these rules, you have a much better chance of molding a child who is always a pleasure to talk to.

In the Car

The Basic Rules:

Listen to the driver • Observe safety routines • Let the driver concentrate • No bathroom talk • If you feel sick, say so • But no crying wolf • Obey family rules

Auto travel for children has changed a lot since our childhood, when seat belts were infrequently used and crowded car pools squashed three or four children into the luggage area of a Ford Country Squire. Sometimes I think juvenile behavior in cars might be a bit better now because kids are forcibly immobilized. But on reflection I doubt that there's been real improvement in noise levels or intensity of bickering.

In defense of children's auto antics, I want to point out that several factors contribute to their antsy behavior. Being confined is one, boredom is another. But I think we also need to take into account that when Mom is driving she is like Mom on the phone—physically present but tantalizingly unavailable. She can't look a child in the eye or be a committed audience to his tale of woe, and this is very frustrating. Naturally enough, attention-getting devices escalate.

But children must behave well in the car because their behavior can affect safety. Anything that distracts the driver from the road should be out of the question. Don't hesitate to demand compliance on this front. The standard method for halting poor behavior is pulling over to the side of the road and turning off the engine until you're satisfied with the level of decorum. If you can accomplish this without losing your temper, it's all the more shocking (in a positive way). I have had to perform this maneuver only once, and it was extremely effective. Six astonished eyes stared at me from the backseat, and for the rest of the trip to school the children barely spoke above a whisper. They were not frightened, mind, but definitely in awe.

There's nothing very complicated or surprising about the ideal behavior of a young passenger. Most children who aren't extremely rowdy will follow these rules automatically. But sometimes they may need to be reminded. If you routinely have trouble with your young passengers, it might be worth taking a bit of extra time one day to write down a list of rules for behavior in the car. (Be sure to solicit their opinions, too; they'll often come up with good suggestions, and their participation in the process helps foster cooperation.) You can copy out your rules neatly with little illustrations and tape them somewhere prominent like the back of the driver's seat, because even non-readers are impressed by the written word. We all spend so much time behind the wheel that it's worth putting a little effort into making that time more pleasant.

Listen to the driver.

Compliance with the grown-up in charge is essential. The best way to be sure your small child will pay attention to Ashley's mom at the wheel is to insist on her paying attention to you.

Observe safety routines.

I am always astonished to see parents get in a car and put a child on their lap. Or fail to insist on a seat belt. The rule in our car is that I don't start the engine until everyone is buckled in. I'm willing to wait as long as I have to for cooperation.

Let the driver concentrate.

My pet peeve is children kicking the back of my seat. Maybe noise levels bother other parents more. Certainly sibling violence in the back is also a great distraction. Kids should know better than to touch the driver or pelt him with spitballs or fire tiny action-figure weapons at him.

No bathroom talk.

Three five-year-olds cooped up in a traffic jam will sooner or later start fighting or talking dirty. At that point the driver says sternly, "No bathroom talk. Jeremy, can you think of a song for us all to sing?" This tactic also works if one of your passengers offends another, which happens pretty easily at this age. "Mrs. Hamlin, Lonnie said my bunny looked dumb!" Then you smoothly cut in with, "Jeremy, can you think of a song. . . ."

If you feel sick, say so.

I was a diffident child, and also extremely prone to motion sickness. It was quite some time before I realized that it was actually better to say, "Mrs. Walker, I feel carsick," than to swallow hard and hope the feeling would go away. Because it never does. And any mother would rather stop and let a kid out than clean a car's upholstery. The same principle is true for needing a bathroom. It wouldn't hurt to point this out in a calm and kindly way before beginning a long trip.

But no crying wolf.

My younger child has inherited my inner-ear difficulties but not my diffidence. I can't tell when he's really feeling ill and when he just wants a little diversion, so I always stop when he claims to be sick. And then sometimes when I get him out of his booster seat he looks at me, pink-cheeked and angelic, and says, "I just needed a little fresh air." If I were not his mother, I would want to throttle him. On the other hand, if I were not his mother, he probably wouldn't be doing it.

Obey family rules.

Some families use rotations to work out who gets to sit in front. Others have bans on eating in the car, while others insist that children keep their hands to themselves (avoiding the possibility of tickle battles). Preschoolers are sophisticated enough to understand the notion of different rules governing different circumstances, including cars. Still, an occasional reminder doesn't hurt. You can say, "Mrs. Grover doesn't let anybody eat in her car so why don't you have a snack before you go." Or "I know Max always sits in front in his car, so do you want to sit in front on the way to his house?"

Older children should always thank the driver as they get out of the car, but I don't expect this of preschoolers. If a child that young takes you for granted, it's really a compliment, because it means she accepts you as part of her world.

Party Manners

My husband never had a birthday party when he was a child. His birthday falls on December 30 and there was just no time in his family's holiday schedule to fit in a party for Rick. He is very proud that he wasn't seriously warped by this deprivation, and when the time came to face the party pressure for our preschool-age son, he thought he could control it. Our children, he decreed, would not have annual birthday parties. Fine, I said skeptically. You explain this to them. Without consulting his father, Willy started planning his fourth birthday party three months ahead of time. Rick backed down. When, six months ahead, Willy started planning his *fifth*, Rick tried to introduce the concept of every-other-year parties. Willy's mind simply rejected the notion. It was inconceivable. Of course you have a birthday party every year!

So we have joined the lockstep parade of parties, and all of them have been an emotional drain. Not one has passed without someone bursting into tears, and it wasn't always me. The pressure on the birthday child is huge, and the emotional temperature for everyone is abnormally high. So from the point of view of manners, I think almost anything is forgivable. These are not normal children we are dealing with, this is not an average situation, and if your generally peaceful and fastidious daughter initiates a food fight with chocolate cake, just take a deep breath and be glad you stocked up on Clorox. You don't want anyone to be mean or to get hurt. Otherwise, the expectations for manners at a preschooler's party are minimal, for guests and host alike.

You have a brief window of opportunity to introduce the manners you'd like to see your child exhibit. Often parents will stay with their children at parties until the little ones are really comfortable in an overexcited mob. By the time your child is five, she'll probably join this mob without a backward glance for you, so while you're still hanging around, try to urge her into these very minimal forms of courtesy.

Greet the guests or host.

Usually kids are so excited to see each other that this is a natural and joyful beginning to the party. The shy may need to be brought forward, though, so they can feel included in the fun. This is easier when numbers are small, but even if the whole class is present, you should forge through the throng to make sure your child says "Hello, happy birthday." If you are the parent of the birthday child and you've been rash enough to invite fifteen four-year-olds to your house, you still have to make sure your child says hello to each guest.

Take turns.

You may see a lot of regressive behavior at a birthday party, but most preschoolers can still manage to wait their turn to have their faces painted or bash the piñata. They may not come to this naturally, but a gentle word from a noncustodial adult ("Martha, honey, Suzanne has been waiting for a long time. Let her go first, then it's your turn") will usually subdue the pushy.

Say "Thank you" when you leave.

This is an entirely parent-prompted activity, of course. As you collect your overheated child, you say, "Now we're going to find Sabrina and thank her for the party. We'll also thank her mother and father." With an older child, you'd probably want to be subtle and whisper in her ear, "Don't forget to say thank you to Mrs. Marvell." But you don't have to worry about embarrassing a five-year-old who's inspecting a goody bag. Just yell over the din, "Say thank you, Andrew," and you'll get credit for having tried.

Otherwise, as adult host or observer, you must be prepared to tolerate all kinds of behavior that would ordinarily horrify you. If nobody is getting hurt, emotionally or physically, try to overlook yelling, inappropriate language, sloppy eating, pushing and shoving as the presents are opened, and grabbing for party bags. Remember, this is the one occasion when singing at the table is appropriate. Everything follows from that.

Thank-You Notes

The Basic Rules:

Preschoolers should send thank-you notes: When presents are not opened under the eye of the giver • When a special grown-up sends a present • When someone gives a child a special treat

A few weeks ago I took Will's second-grade class on a field trip. This involved a couple of hours of my time, sitting through a performance of shadow puppets. It was perfectly pleasant and I'm sure I would have forgotten it right away except that in Will's backpack when he came home was a thank-you note from the whole class. It said, "Dear Ms. Hamlin [my married name], Thank you for coming with us to Symphony Space to see 'The African Drum.'" All the children had signed it and there was a pretty design of flowered vines at the top of the page. And it made me feel *appreciated*.

I am recounting this not entirely fascinating anecdote in detail because I feel very strongly about thank-you notes and I want to stress their most important characteristic: They make the recipients feel terrific. And the natural consequence of that is very warm feelings toward the author of a thank-you note. Let me spell it out for you. People like children who write thank-you notes.

Now let's step back into reality. It's three days after your five-year-old daughter's birthday. There were twelve little girls at her party, and half of the new Barbie accessories have already been lost. There were also presents from aunts and uncles, grandparents, and the lady who lives next door who doesn't have any grandchildren. And, of course, your daughter can't write. So what are you supposed to do? Do you have to write twenty thank-you notes yourself?

No. Not unless everyone you know does so (in which case you don't need any advice from me about how, when, or whether to write them). When children are very small, you do need to introduce them to the concept of writing a letter of thanks, but they are really too young for you to be worrying about forming this habit yet. So you really have to write notes only in the following circumstances:

When presents are not opened under the eye of the giver.

For instance, if you give a birthday party and choose not to open the gifts on the spot, you need to send notes to let the donors know that their gifts were received and appreciated. The same is true, and even more necessary, for gifts that come in the mail. Otherwise you risk getting that phone call that goes, "Did Russell get my little package . . . ?" If you've ever sent a gift that wasn't acknowledged, you know how annoying it is to wonder if it was received and if the recipient liked it. I cannot stress enough how important I think this is.

When a special grown-up sends a present.

You know who they are for your family: godparents, grandparents, really close friends. Anyone over 60, in particular, may expect to be thanked on paper for a gift. Naturally this means that if they aren't, they will feel huffy and neglected. Don't take the chance. Write the note.

When someone gives a child a special treat.

Your friend Laura took Josie to tea at the Plaza to see where Eloise grew up. Or your son's best friend's family took him camping. You'll recognize these occasions when they come up. You'll feel incredibly grateful. Put some of that gratitude on paper, even if you see the treat-giver frequently.

Mind you, these thank-you notes need not be impeccable missives on the best engraved paper, written with a black fountain pen in perfect script. Nor need they be long. Nor even particularly original. I've seen lots of clever or cute or funny ways to express thanks in the name of, or with the assistance of, a preschooler.

The most traditional form would probably be a note that's frankly from the parent, saying something like, "Colin just loves the hiking boots you sent him. . . ." There's a lot more spontaneity and charm, though, in a creation that involves your child. What's more, there is no need in the world to spend a lot of time on this unless it's pouring rain outside and you can't get anybody to come over for a play date. Here are a few ideas:

- Use postcards. We collect them and let the boys pick which they want to send. I usually write a short message that Timo then "signs" in letters about four inches high.

- Use a computer artwork program. After a birthday party you could compose one basic note that can be altered to apply to each gift. Your child can then decorate or color it.

- Send one of your child's drawings, which you've written a message on.

- Use photos. A friend of mine puts all of her mediocre snapshots into her children's art box, and they use them in collages. What better image to put on a thank-you note than your own child's smiling (if somewhat blurry) face?

- Keep the message really short. "Sam loves the stuffed tiger," written on a piece of typing paper with a couple of stickers and a crayon scribble or two, is perfectly fine.

- Avoid using glitter on notes to people who don't have children. They may not like picking it out of their rugs.

• RESISTANCE FIGHTERS •

Most of the time, children need reminders because they've honestly forgotten the manners you're trying to teach them. These are habits, after all, and habits take a while to learn. But there are also times in kids' lives when they are simply prone to resist any suggestion, from "I think you'll need mittens" to "Could you put your napkin in your lap?"

With a two-year-old, you need to save your energy for the big battles, like holding hands when you cross the street. But during the phases when your child is generally more biddable, he will still occasionally dig in his heels about manners issues. These are often power struggles, and here are a few tips for dealing with them:

Allow the child to save face.

Can you give her an element of control in the situation? If she can't bring herself to shake hands with a grown-up, for instance, a wave will do.

Build in a reward if possible.

We had trouble getting our four-year-old to clear his place after dinner. It became a lot easier when he took his plate to the sink before dessert, so that dessert was his reward. (Okay, sometimes we have to threaten that he won't get his cookies. . . .) And it's not a "bribe." It's a "positive consequence."

Ask his opinion.

As early as five, kids can have very practical notions about how to accomplish things. Explain the situation: six thank-you notes to produce this weekend. And turn it over to him: Does he want to do them all at once, or two at a time? Kids comply much better with rules they helped to draft.

Stand firm.

If you crumble on manners conflicts, you send the message that this stuff isn't that important after all. We've endured sulks and weeping and slammed doors and black clouds of emotional atmosphere sparked off by "little" things like the loser throwing around the Candy Land cards. Better your kids should blow up at you than at a prospective mother-in-law.

TV Guide

Ask before turning on the TV • Consult anyone else who's watching before changing channels • Keep the noise level bearable • Sit so everyone else can see

How often and how much your child watches TV is not manners, so it's not my business. But *how* she watches TV is. These are all basic, obvious guidelines, and if a child doesn't stick to them she'll get beaned by an older sibling. (Or, later on, by a friend, roommate, or spouse.) Still, for the record, children need to:

Ask before turning on the TV.

Especially in someone else's house. You can loosen up on this a little later on, when older children are watching a show they've discussed with you beforehand. But it's obnoxious for a five-year-old to wander into the living room and flick on the soaps in the middle of a play date.

Consult anyone else who's watching before changing channels.

Channel surfing with a four-year-old can be really disconcerting. Only the most precocious preschoolers will try this, though older siblings may teach the younger ones about the wonders of the remote control device. You don't have to worry too much about enforcing this rule since peer pressure will probably take care of it for you.

Keep the noise level bearable.

Grown-ups get to decide what's bearable. If you sense the volume inching up as soon as you leave the room, you can turn the TV off to show that you're serious.

Sit so everybody else can see.

Again, peer pressure is the enforcer.

Now I realize that the whole point of letting your children watch TV is so that you can get out of each other's hair for a while. You may want to poke your head in to make sure they aren't watching *Bloody Cannibal Combat*, but you shouldn't intervene otherwise. And if your child can follow the rules above, you won't need to.

The Name Game

Call grown-ups "Mr." or "Mrs." when you first meet them.

No area of manners makes me more nervous than the question of what my children should call adults. It was simple when we were growing up: They were all "Mr. Black" or "Mrs. White." But now that *we're* the grown-ups, the issue is more complicated.

I was trying to figure out if our new teenage baby-sitter should call me Mrs. Hamlin. It's my married name, the name of my children. But I just couldn't imagine being comfortable hearing Nicole say, "Mrs. Hamlin, what should I give the boys for dinner?" Because I don't feel like Mrs. Hamlin. Despite all the evidence, gray hair and mortgage and station wagon, I cannot grasp the fact that I'm a grown-up. I know I'm not fourteen, thank God, but I couldn't *possibly* be forty! No matter what my driver's license says.

I think this is where a lot of first-name use for kids comes from. Many other parents out there are also resisting adulthood. And there's another point: Women who didn't take their husband's name often dislike having it used. So what are they supposed to do: Cringe when they hear it, but let it go? Politely suggest that children call them "Mrs. Grey?" Or let kids use their first names?

Some of you are no doubt lucky enough to live in a town where the standards are perfectly clear. Lots of children still use "Mr." and "Mrs." automatically. Other children call most adults, including their teachers, "Joe" and "Barbara." But lots of us belong to several communities where the standards are different: first names at the preschool, last names at the grade school, for instance. (Don't worry about confusion: Small kids will accept the inconsistency without question.) You can't go wrong, though, if you teach your children the following system.

Call grown-ups "Mr." or "Mrs." when you first meet them.

There are three very good reasons for using last names. First, you avoid offending people who are accustomed to having children use their titles and a last name. Second, this formality gives the grown-up a little bit of extra authority. I've noticed that many of my friends who are teachers, for instance, insist on last names. And finally, if your child develops a warm relationship with this adult, the grown-up can always say, "Johnny, I wish you'd call me Anna instead of Mrs. Nordstrom." Which is a pleasant compliment.

As a parent, you need to take a couple of steps to support this habit. The first one is to make sure your children know what name to use. That means introducing people clearly, or jogging your child's memory if you need to. "Henry, you remember Mr. Churchill, don't you?" If you're meeting someone for the first time and you don't know their last name, ask what it is. Say you've just been introduced to Tony. "Hi, Tony," you say, "it's nice to meet you. This is my son Walter. Walter, this is . . . what's your last name, Tony?" Tony says Gruen. "This is Mr. Gruen." And Walter (see "Meeting Adults," page 13) puts out his hand and says, "Hi, Mr. Gruen." It may be awkward at first but it will get easier and easier. Sometimes you will meet grown-ups who prefer to have their first names used, but that's their choice, and they need to make it clear to you. An effective variation on this ploy is to ask outright, "What do you like children to call you?" I tend to take this route when introducing my sons to women so that I won't blunder over "Miss/ Ms./Mrs."

Aside from finding out what people's last names and preferred titles are, you also need to use them. If you want grown-ups to be

"Mr. and Mrs." to your children, refer to them that way in family conversations. "Mr. Parks is giving us a ride to the library." "I had lunch with Mrs. Weiss today." I remember thinking it was odd that my parents always talked about exciting things that happened to Joan and Sam and Sally: pipes bursting or relatives dying or the lawnmower blowing up. And they had this whole other set of friends, Mr. and Mrs. Nevis and Mr. and Mrs. Shawn, and all *they* did was carpool and come over for dinner. It took me years to discover that they were the same set of people.

I don't think our generation is ever going to get back to that level of formality, but we may have gotten too casual about names. If you get into the pattern of using last names until the adult in question suggests otherwise, you really can't go wrong.

• CALL ME MOM! •

When children reach a certain stage around the age of three, they suddenly realize that everybody has a first name and a last name, maybe even a middle name. Even parents! In other words, old Mom and Dad have given names that other people use for them. When my younger son discovered this, he decided that he, too, wanted to call me Carol.

For some reason, this rubbed me the wrong way. It seemed disrespectful, even though most of his friends use my first name. I felt my authority diminish. "Mom" is unique, "Mom" is powerful, but telephone salesmen whom I've never met call me Carol.

So I nipped it in the bud. We were parking the car on the way home from school. I knelt on the sidewalk next to the car and put my hands on his elbows. "I am *Mom*," I pronounced gravely. "You and Willy are the only people in the *whole world* who can call me that." He blinked. This was a big idea to grasp. "So you call me Mom, or Mommy. Because you're the only ones who can."

It seems to have worked for now. I expect a recurrence in about a dozen years, though.

Private Behavior

Nose-picking is private behavior • Picking teeth is private behavior • Masturbation is private behavior • Say "Excuse me" when you burp

If manners are your presentation to the world, then they aren't just limited to speech or even to interactions with other people. There are also standards for handling one's own body that don't come naturally to most children. They have to be taught, and the preschool years are the time to do it. I don't think many people really object to a three-year-old whipping her skirt up over her head in the middle of the supermarket. That's completely innocent and inoffensive. On the other hand, Timo came home from school one day when he was four, dropped his shorts and shouted "Baby butt!" when that part of his anatomy appeared. Clearly unacceptable.

I would make a distinction here between unconscious habits that our society frowns on (nose-picking, for instance) and behavior designed to provoke a reaction. You can tell which is which with your own child. Timothy's defiant grin when he's showing me his bottom tips me off that he's just jangling my chain. And of course the appropriate reaction in a situation like this is to make the limits of behavior very clear to your child. No, you keep your clothes on. No, we don't talk about butts. Period.

But we need to be a little more gentle with the kinds of physical explorations that kids are prone to but polite society prefers not to witness. None of us wants to make our children self-conscious about completely natural functions. The urge for modesty and privacy will set in soon enough anyway. When your daughter is nine and you're breaking a trail in the trackless wilderness outside your campsite to find her a *really* private place to pee, you'll probably think back with some fondness to the days when you couldn't get her to keep her clothes on. In the meantime, our conventions regarding our bodies are as follows:

Nose-picking is private behavior.

I have known girls as young as five who were capable of extracting tissues from those tiny packets, blowing their noses, and throwing the used tissue away in an available receptacle. More common, I think, is direct excavation or perhaps the announcement to an adult (usually when she's on the phone and cooking dinner at the same time), "Mom, I need a tissue." Even though there are boxes of tissues at a child's eye level in every room of the house. You will have to tell your child over and over again that nobody wants to see her explore her nasal cavities (although many children, with infallible timing, seem to be prompted to pick their noses only when they're in large groups or on stage). Hand her a tissue and send her off to the bathroom with the instructions, "And wash your hands afterward." This is also a good place for a lecture on transmission of germs.

Picking teeth is private behavior.

A child chews and swallows. Why should he stop there? There's a whole meal left in the crevices of his molars. So he digs it out, then wipes his fingers on his shirt. Yecch! This particular uncouthness is really hard to stop once it takes root, so watch carefully and nip it in the bud. You can suggest taking several swallows of milk, or even, somewhat drastically, you can excuse a child to go pick his teeth in the bathroom. The sociable will correctly regard this as exile and refuse, in which case you need to stand firm on the picking ban. As a last resort, you could try suspending consumption of the offending foods. (Grape-Nuts? Popcorn?) Or point out that maybe he should do some extra flossing.

Masturbation is private behavior.

You don't want to discourage a child's exploring his or her sexual nature, but it will make most witnesses uncomfortable. Many parenting experts suggest gently telling a child, "That's something we do in private." Reminders may be necessary, but it's important not to embarrass the child. For some kids masturbation is a comfort ritual much like thumb-sucking. That makes it harder to discourage, but it is something kids will outgrow in time. If you don't place any more emphasis on it than you would on nose-picking, you won't inadvertently convey any negative messages about sex.

Say "Excuse me" when you burp.

After you spend all those months whacking your baby on the back to bring up the air, it's easy to forget that ours is not a culture that uses burps to express satisfaction. Very small children can't help burping, but if you laugh at them they will pretend to burp for the next twenty minutes, so the burden is on you to keep your face straight or dive under the table to tie your shoe until your composure is restored. Burping on command is of course one of the greatly prized skills of childhood, but you must make it very clear that audiences over twelve no longer appreciate it.

Ideally, a child who burps or farts will quietly say "Excuse me" and everyone else will ignore the event. Childish grown-ups often fail to live up to this standard, but it should be presented as a goal.

• Y A W N •

It is polite to cover your mouth when you yawn. I think there are a couple of reasons for this. One has to do with the unprepossessing nature of the gaping jaw and the interior of the human mouth. The other has to do with the fact that yawns often indicate boredom, and the truly polite person is never bored.

It's not necessary to tell this to a child. All you have to say is, "Sweetie, can you cover your mouth when you yawn? Just like you cover your mouth when you cough." If your child wants to know why, just open your own mouth really wide and say, "Look. Is that pretty?"

Audience Participation

The Basic Rules:

Stay in your seat • Don't kick the seat in front of you
• Don't talk • Don't eat or drink

I'm not really sure this section belongs in Part I of the book because I'm not really sure that children under the age of six should be taken to formal live performances. Sitting still and paying attention for at least forty-five minutes straight is a big strain for a small child. Not talking for the same length of time is virtually impossible, and many children just can't whisper.

On the other hand, there's something really wonderful about exposing small children to the magic of the stage or concert hall. If you look around any *Nutcracker* audience around Christmastime, some of the most awe-struck faces are those of the smallest kids. It's your call, of course. If you do decide to take your preschooler to the theater, the folks in the seats nearby will thank you for insisting on the following behavior. And remember, if you have any doubt that your child can behave this discreetly, wait a while. The *Nutcracker* comes back every year.

Stay in your seat.

Your child's place in the audience is either in the seat you paid for, or in your lap. Not standing up and breathing down the neck of the person in front of him. Or kneeling backward in his seat, staring at the people behind him. Or in the aisle, tripping the ushers. I think sightlines matter less to really small children than a degree of mobility, so the front row of a box or balcony can be a good choice. At least if your child stands up, he won't be bothering anybody in front of him, and he's small enough not to block the view.

Don't underestimate the difficulty of keeping an energetic child in one place. There's a lot more latitude for wiggling at performances geared to young audiences, but a really antsy child is hugely irritating to everyone around her.

Don't kick the seat in front of you.

I didn't really have to spell that out, did I?

Don't talk.

I have a brochure here from New York's Little Orchestra Society that says, "encourage your child to wait until the concert is over to ask questions or make comments." I don't think there's a five-year-old alive who witnesses a live performance without asking questions ("Mommy, how does the lady make that wobbly noise with her voice?"). What you can do is insist on whispers, remind the child you aren't supposed to be talking, and keep your answers really short.

Don't eat or drink.

Don't even chew gum. The bane of every concert hall is the slowly unwrapped peppermint in crackly paper, but chewing on pretzels is also inappropriate. The whole point of live performance is that the audience should be focused entirely on what's happening on stage. Not on the taste sensation provided by a chocolate chip cookie. Providing distraction from the performers is inconsiderate. Any child can manage to refrain from eating for an hour. If you're worried about this, give your child a snack just before you take your seats. And then if he says he's hungry halfway through, you'll know that you have a problem, but not the one he thinks. Because he's actually bored.

Once you get your child accustomed to these restrictions, he'll be ready to join the stuffiest audience anywhere. (He'll probably be better behaved than half of the grown-ups in the average auditorium, but you don't have to tell him that.)

• N A G ,   N A G ,   N A G •

I spend as much time as the next mother reminding my children what I expect of them. In fact maybe as much as twenty percent of what I say to them on any given day may be directives about their behavior. (That would be a pretty bad day, I admit.) But I do not consider myself a nag. I honestly think I'm more like a coach, the Manners Coach.

Imagine how helpful it would be if from time to time a kindly voice spoke in your ear, issuing helpful or encouraging advice: "The flame is on too high under the spaghetti sauce." "Don't forget to pay the phone bill." "You were very smart to check the oil in the car." If you're careful to offer praise as frequently as you issue reminders, it's easy to communicate to your child that you're working together on learning manners and, furthermore, doing a very good job.

PART II

The Age of Reason

Ages 6-9

A lot of the politeness we try to instill in a preschooler involves teaching that child how to manage himself: how not to bully friends when they come over to play, how to eat without disgusting everybody, how to wait in a line, and how to sit quietly during a concert.

School-age children, from six through nine, are moving into the social years. Having mastered the basics of self-control, they move on to the more complicated matters of amiable interactions with other people, both children and adults. Older children do things that smaller kids don't usually do, like sleep over at their friends' houses. And we expect more poise and awareness of other people from them. You wouldn't be annoyed at a four-year-old who slammed into you in the supermarket, but you expect an eight-year-old to watch where she's going. In fact, a lot of behavior that was tolerable in a five-year-old will suddenly seem annoying in an older child.

In many respects it's easier to teach children manners when they get to be six or seven. I called this section "The Age of Reason" because kids make a quantum leap in development around first grade. They sometimes remember what you've told them, even if you said it only once. And they don't test you anywhere near as much. Their ability to empathize is pretty solid, too, so if you say, "Cecily feels terrible when you tease her about her birthmark," they understand.

In fact, these are prime years to work on teaching good manners. If you've laid the groundwork as I suggest in Part I, your child will already be tuned in to the desirability of being polite. But even if you're starting afresh, a lot of these concepts will sink in quite readily. You'll need to go back and work on the rules in Part I, because they're the building blocks. And, yes, some of the polite behavior we expect of older children does require the hard work of forming good habits (especially at the table). But kids in elementary school are eager to master the world. They're old enough to know that there are right and wrong ways to do things, and they want to do them right. If you can introduce a new set of polite behaviors along with a new experience, your child has a powerful incentive to remember what you've told him. So before he goes on his first sleepover, you run through the sleepover rules. Or you say to your daughter, "Emily, would you like to be in charge of answering the phone? This is what you need to do." And run through the rules.

The challenge in teaching courtesy to children of this age is that they spend so much time apart from their parents. You really hope, for instance, that your son thanks the driver every time the car pool drops him off at school. But you aren't there to remind him. You hope your daughter clears her place when she has dinner at her father's house. And that she would get out of the way of a lady with a cane while she's walking to school. Often all you can do is insist on mannerly behavior while you're around and slip in an occasional reminder. And remember, children always save their worst behavior for their parents.

• GREAT EXPECTATIONS •

Think about what social situations make you uncomfortable. Meeting people, elaborate meals, phone calls with strangers? Usually it's the unknown that alarms us. I always wonder if I should stand up when I'm introduced to someone, and whether I should shake hands, and all too often I worry so much that I don't catch the person's name. I don't know what's expected of me and that makes me confused and uncomfortable.

Kids feel the same way, but parents can help. Be sure your children know what they're going to encounter in a new situation. "We're going to your sister's school to see a play and you'll need to remember not to talk during the play. And afterward we'll go to a party in her classroom and you can give her a hug and eat some cookies. A few cookies. Three." Or "When you come to my office a lot of people will want to meet you. I'll tell you their names and you can shake hands with them. I bet a lot of them will say how big you are."

Wouldn't it be nice to have somebody do the same for you?

Meeting People

Intermediate Rules:

Tell your parent your friend's name • Tell your friend
your parent's name

If you've managed to teach your child the principles outlined in "Meeting Adults" in Part I, you're no stranger to the look of pleasure on people's faces when they first encounter your courteous child. The simple routine of saying hello and shaking hands while looking someone in the eye would get even a politician successfully through a long day of campaigning.

But polite people also need to learn how to perform introductions. Most of us feel awkward about this. I'm sure you can think of a dozen situations when you failed to introduce people because you couldn't think of how to do it, or else did introduce them only to be told that they'd been roommates in college. On the other hand, it's even worse to stand next to a friend who has just run into an acquaintance and not be introduced. It's suddenly as if you didn't exist.

The awkwardness we feel during introductions may never vanish, but a routine reduces it enormously, for children as well as adults, and you can help your child by establishing this routine. Bring it up some time in a casual way: "I'd like you to learn how to introduce your friends to me," and explain what's involved. The next time you introduce an adult to your child, point out afterward that that's how you'd like her to handle your meeting her friends. Remind her, in a whisper but not out loud, the next time you encounter a pal of hers whom you don't know.

The actual procedure is not complicated. What's more, it doesn't need to be smooth, not at first. You don't care if your child chokes or stumbles on the names, and his friends don't either. All he needs to say are two sentences.

Tell your parent your friend's name.

"Mom, this is Bart."

Tell your friend your parent's name.

"Bart, this is my stepfather, Peter." Or "my mother, Dr. Skolnick." Or whatever. If he starts out with just, "This is my mom," he has still done Bart a courteous service by identifying you, since in today's complicated families there's no telling who that grown-up in the kitchen might be.

If you thank your child each time he performs an introduction, and occasionally comment on how comfortable it makes everyone feel, you'll encourage a courteous practice. And in time, it will become an extremely attractive habit.

• JUST DIFFERENT •

I don't like the new language we use for people's differences: Phrases like "challenged" and "differently abled" seem clumsy. But when you're trying to explain different abilities or physical quirks to a child, these terms are a real gift. They're still clumsy, but they help you discuss Nature's inequities without using pejorative terms. And you need to discuss them, because these are facts of life. Most of us have ten fingers and ten toes but some of us don't. Most of us can walk without assistance, but some of us can't. Most of us can read pretty well by second grade, but some of us aren't able to. Different isn't bad: It's just not the same. And every human being must be respected, regardless of her capabilities. So children must never, ever, tease or laugh at someone because of a disability, permanent or temporary. That's not just rude, it's cruel.

Teaching empathy is essential. "How would you feel if . . .?" Kids understand that and they're usually ready to show some sympathy. What's a little harder to handle is children's curiosity about different abilities or physical features. Often, what they want to know is practical. Last spring Timo broke his leg, so he was in a body cast for a month. He was quite a sight, encased in fiberglass from ribcage to ankle, and some of his pals found the cast a bit intimidating. But once they'd knocked on it and ascertained that Timo was really in there and that he'd come out soon, all they wanted to know was, "How do you pee?" And once he'd shown them the pee bottle, they were ready to play with him.

It's very easy to hurt people's feelings with blunt questions, though. A child might offend a dwarf by asking how tall she was, while a man in a wheelchair might gladly demonstrate how the gears work. (Children should be taught, by the way, never to touch or talk to a working seeing-eye dog.) The safest rule is that children should never make personal remarks about other people's differences, or ask direct questions about them. It's hard to instill tact in a preschooler, but a child of six and up can be taught to keep her observations and curiosity to herself for a while, especially if she has a little warning. As in, "We're going to the Lymers'. You don't know them, but Mr. Lymer has only one leg. I'm telling you this now so you won't stare at him, because he might feel shy about it." Children whose tact has been awakened can be very discreet, so preparation can be quite gentle.

Of course you won't always have the chance to prepare your child for meeting someone with physical differences, but a whispered appeal for empathy followed up by an explanation will usually guarantee the considerate response you want.

Table Manners

Intermediate Rules:

Come to the table with clean hands and face • Bow your head if a blessing is said • Hold the fork like a pencil • Don't hold your fork in your fist when you cut food • Take small bites • Don't wash food down with drinks • Don't gulp drinks • Use your napkin discreetly • Ask, don't grab • Taste every food • Don't criticize the food • Put your knife and fork together at the end of the meal • Don't eat and run

Table manners are probably the most complex set of behaviors kids have to learn, and the most unnatural. You can't trust to empathy, sensitivity, and good intentions to get you through dinner, because so many of our customs have their roots in the Middle Ages, when social circumstances didn't look much like ours.

Not that kids care. But by the time they reach the age of six, you may be able to get them interested in the foundations of some of our polite customs, particularly if you stress that armed combat was a constant threat hundreds of years ago. To this day, we set our tables with the blade of the knife facing the plate because back then a jumpy or hostile neighbor might take offense at sitting next to the business side of something that could be used as a weapon.

You can also point out that nobody ever got to be a knight until his manners were perfect. Also that knights competed to attract ladies with their shows of courtly behavior. And further, that at the age of eight or so young boys were sent away from home to be squires in someone else's home. One of the things they were taught was how to behave with courtesy. In other words, even back in the Middle Ages kids had to learn manners, but at least your children get to do it at home. (If you keep getting grief about the learning process you can always offer to send your children to their grandmother's to learn how to eat politely.)

Learning table manners is a cumulative process. A child in grade school should know the basics. At the very least, she should sit at the table, use utensils, chew with her mouth closed, and refrain from talking until she has swallowed. That doesn't mean that all of these things are going to happen at once, but at least she'll know what you're talking about when you say, "Chew and swallow before you talk, please."

But there are new skills to be acquired, too. I wouldn't dump these on a child all at once, but introduce them gradually, as you did with the manners in Part I. Concentrate on one or two issues at a time, and try to overlook the shortcomings. Margaret Kelly, author of *The Family Almanac*, suggests dressing up family dinners with candles and wine once or twice a week. The candles, she says, ensure that you see less of your children's misbehavior, and the wine makes you care less about it.

Come to the table with clean hands and face.

Taking the trouble to arrive at meals in a presentable state demonstrates respect for the people you're going to sit down with. Also, gray fingermarks on the apple slices may put other people off their food. I don't think there's a child in America who would scrub his hands without prompting, so you have to build this step into the dinner routine. I find it works best to give successive warnings. About ten minutes before I think we'll want to sit down, I let the boys know that it's time to finish reading that page or to throw three more passes. Then five minutes before dinner, I start to shoo them toward the sink. Then I generally have to do some stamping around and shouting, but they do eventually converge on the table with clean hands.

Bow your head if a blessing is said.

This indicates respect for the household deity, whoever that may be. It also prevents anyone from jumping the gun and eating before everyone is served.

Hold the fork like a pencil.

Children in grade school have enough manual dexterity to master the correct grip (see "Pencil vs. Hose," page 79). I know it seems petty, but there are people in the world who may, in the future, judge your little darling harshly if he holds his fork in his fist like a club. If you take care of this now, he'll only have to worry about getting soup on his tie at that crucial job interview in twenty years.

Don't hold your fork in your fist when you cut food.

Think, for a minute, about how hard it is to get the meat off your average chicken breast. You have to hold the thing down while trying to scrape the meat away from the bones. If you did this in a lab you'd call it dissecting, and you'd be able to use your fingers. No wonder a lot of parents still cut meat for their nine-year-olds; learning to cut food properly is a lot of work. What's more, there are two ways you can do it: the American style or the European style.

This is the kind of finicky issue that gives manners a bad name. Americans traditionally cut food by steadying the piece of ham (for example) with the fork, held in the left hand, tines down. The knife, held in the right hand, cuts off a bite-size piece. When the food is cut, the knife is then placed at the side of the plate and the fork is switched to the right hand for eating.

This is very complicated and awkward. The other way to manage is the European method, which involves the same system for cutting (knife in right hand, fork tines down in left hand). But instead of putting down the knife and switching the fork back to the right hand, you impale food on the fork in your left hand and eat it that way, without turning the fork over. In other words, the fork travels to your mouth with the convex curve of the tines upward. (Some experts say that left-handers are supposed to reverse these procedures, but I'm left-handed and I've never held a fork in my right hand. I think this is one instance when things could actually be simpler for southpaws.)

The advantage of the European method is that you can use your knife as a pusher and really get your bites solidly fixed onto that fork before it gets to your mouth. On the other hand there are foods (peas, for instance) that are really hard to eat unless you scoop them up. Using the European method you would have to spear them on the tines of the fork or else mash them onto the back of the fork with something a little more adhesive like, say, meatloaf. The advantage of the American style is that once you get your meat cut, you can pick it up on your fork the normal way, and even slip on a blob of mashed potatoes if you want.

I don't actually believe that many people are going to notice how your children eat and decide that they're socially unacceptable because they switch their fork back and forth. Managing with confidence and skill matter much more. So you can offer your kids the choice of methods and let them practice until they're adept. It's a good idea to start with easier foods like ground meat and large ravioli. You can graduate to the stuff with bones a little later on.

Take small bites.

A bite of food should be small enough to fit comfortably in the mouth without stretching the cheeks. What's more, it should be chewable with the lips closed. You could actually perform an experiment. Let your child try out various sizes of bite. Yes, he can fit an entire Oreo into his mouth at once. No, he can't chew it without losing a few crumbs. So it does not qualify as a small bite.

Children haven't yet been socialized to find overflowing mouths unattractive. For most of them, time spent at the table eating is time not spent playing, so they want to get that food into their stomachs as fast as possible. As a parent, you need to slow them down, and since you're working against a natural instinct, you'll have to remind them again and again until the unnatural practice of eating slowly becomes habit.

Don't wash food down with drinks.

It may never occur to your child to open a mouthful of half-chewed hot dog and take a swallow of milk. But if it does, you'll want to stop this behavior before it settles in. You can explain to your child that, ideally, the mouth opens once to accept a mouthful of food and then doesn't open again until the whole mouthful has been swallowed.

Don't gulp drinks.

At the table, drinks should be swallowed one or two mouthfuls at a time. If they are drunk faster than that, there shouldn't be any accompanying noises. No glugging in the throat, no sigh of satisfaction afterward. No wrist drawn across the mouth to wipe off the milk mustache. (Remember napkins?) I doubt that telling someone *not* to do something after they've just done it is the most effective form of discipline. It probably makes more sense to interrupt a child in mid-gulp and point out that you're not on the sidelines of a sporting event and that's not Gatorade in the cup and you hope he's not planning on pouring the leftovers over his head when he's finished.

Use your napkin discreetly.

It's not quite enough that your child merely use his napkin. It has to be done delicately. A napkin is not a bath towel and shouldn't be dragged across the lower half of the face as if someone were trying to remove clown makeup. A corner of the napkin is applied to the edges of the mouth, ideally after each bite or sip. You can alternate vocal reminders with pantomime to keep your child on track.

Ask, don't grab.

If the ketchup is three feet down the table, a child's instinct will be to scoot herself up on her chair and reach, usually without considering that her T-shirt is grazing her plate and her elbow is dangerously close to her brother's milk. Even without stains and spills, this technique isn't ideal. She should say, "Tom, could you please pass me the ketchup?" There are different ways to make this request, like "Gimme the ketchup," or "I need ketchup," or even, "Where's the ketchup?" but they're all as bad as reaching.

What makes this lesson hard to impart is its inconsistency. Parents keep trying to get children to do things for themselves—tie their shoes, find the hairbrush, pour a drink—instead of making us do it for them. So there is genuine illogic here. When the ketchup is within reach, why not get it? I think this tradition probably comes from the days when servants waited on table and the polite diner sat perfectly helpless, asking for whatever he needed. The concept of helplessness shouldn't be too hard for the average child to grasp.

It's up to you to decide *how* politely helpless you want your kids to be during meals. Although it's annoying to be constantly hopping up and down from the table to get things, I'd rather do that than have *them* hopping up and down. And imagine them at a friend's dinner table. Wouldn't you rather Vanessa said, "Could I please have some more milk?" instead of just getting up and helping herself?

Taste every food.

Gone are the days of the clean plate club. Modern-day wisdom is that children are more likely to acquire eating problems if they're forced to eat. This is one of those differences that makes our parents furious. "When you were a kid you ate all your spinach!" they'll thunder. Well, fine, but that's not the way we do it nowadays.

It is still good manners, though, to taste everything on your plate. And stoically to disguise any feelings of revulsion. Cutting food into small bits and spreading it artistically around the plate may fool a very few (childless) hostesses into thinking you've eaten more than you have.

Don't criticize the food.

"The juice is too pulpy." "I don't like the brown parts." "It tastes funny." Even if the cook has done nothing more elaborate than open a box and punch a few buttons on the microwave, the non-cooks must not complain about the food. They don't have to eat it all, but they can certainly maintain what's known as a "diplomatic silence" about its shortcomings. If your child does tend to criticize your cooking, it's time for a little talk. "I worked hard to make that soup and it makes me feel terrible when you tell me what's wrong with it. You don't have to finish it, but don't complain about it." You're not trying to make her feel guilty, you're just being straight with her.

Put your knife and fork together at the end of the meal.

This is the well-known international symbol for "I'm ready for dessert." If you serve dessert to anyone whose knife and fork are placed correctly, and overlook anyone whose utensils are lying around all anyhow, you'll make your point easily. "Oh, I'm sorry," you say, feigning surprise as you look at the plate. "I didn't think you were ready."

Don't eat and run.

You're doing well to get a preschooler to sit down for fifteen or twenty minutes at the table. But an older child is capable of sitting for a longer time, waiting for the adults to finish or even participating in the conversation. One way to achieve this behavior is to ask your child a question just as she's putting her knife and fork together. "How did the spelling test go?" or "Did Lisa get the puppy?" or "Do you think the Bulls have a chance at the title this year?" You may get a lecture, but that's at least a step on the way toward the ideal of stimulating dinner-table conversation.

All these rules seem like a lot to teach. Sometimes I look at my eight-year-old and think, "He can't cut his food without mangling it. He eats as if he were never going to see another meal. He never once wipes his mouth unless I tell him to." But then I realize he is only eight, and cutting food neatly is a skill, and he *has* learned to chew with his mouth closed and keep his elbows off the table, so there is obviously hope. Most important, he seems to understand that mealtimes are not just fueling stops, but also pleasant occasions to exchange news with other members of the family. And that's the biggest lesson of all.

• PENCIL VERSUS HOSE •

When children are just starting to use utensils, it's natural for them to grab the handles in their fists. But by the age of six, it's time to correct that grip. I tried demonstrating, and I tried bending the small fingers into the correct position (very disruptive to mealtime), but what worked best was the "pencil or hose" analogy. The "hose" grip is the full fist; the "pencil" grip is the correct one. And because it's already familiar to children, you can issue a telegraphic reminder when they forget, as they will, and start scooping up the Cheerios in the familiar, uncouth fashion. The suggestion may spark some silliness—a fork/hose pretending to spray the table with spaghetti sauce—but that makes it all the more memorable.

Manners of Speech

Intermediate Rules:

Speak when you're spoken to • No whispering •
No muttering • Don't be a smart aleck • Don't con-
tradict • Avoid insults • Say "You're welcome" when
someone thanks you • When someone says "How
are you?" answer, "Fine, thanks, how are you?" •
Say "I'm sorry" when you bump into someone

Children's capacities with language grow constantly. This is
generally a thrilling thing for parents to observe, as vocabula-
ries blossom and the concepts expressed become ever more
subtle. But there are aspects of this development that can
be exasperating or downright rude.

Part of what's happening in these early school years is a shift in
your child's identity. School and peers take on increasing importance. At the same time, kids are exposed to much more, and a lot
of it is stuff parents wouldn't necessarily approve of (the songs they
sing at the back of the school bus, for instance). I think it's perfectly
appropriate for kids to have these innocuous secrets. They're traveling on the long road to differentiation from you, and using words
you don't use—or knowing words they think you don't know—is
an important part of that process. Hence the origin of teen slang.

But you don't have to hear nasty language at the dinner table.

The key to keeping speech presentable at this (or any) age is
constant vigilance. Using certain words or expressions can become
habits, and there are bound to be some expressions you don't want
to hear. Nip them in the bud. Use a gentle explanation the first time
they crop up and be prepared to remind and remind. Willy came

home from camp one day saying "Yo!" every fourth word. "Yo! Mom! Can I have some milk?" Yo, my foot! I sat down and explained that this was not the way we talked to people. Especially not to grown-ups. And for the next few days, every time I heard "Yo!"— it was amazing how fast it had taken root—I asked him to rephrase what he'd said. Generally this involved using somebody's name, as in, "John, do you want to trade Roberto Clemente for Rickey Henderson?" instead of, "Yo! do you want to trade. . . ." Big improvement.

Feel free to provide alternatives to your child as well. I know a nine-year-old who currently thinks that everything "sucks." Not that he really knows what it means. Every time he utters the dread sibilant his mother stops him and asks what he really wants to say. The movie sucked. Was it boring, or scary, or too babyish? The bagel sucks. Too chewy? Too crusty? Disgusting? Some children enjoy vivid vocabulary, and if you offer a picturesque word or phrase ("I think cartoons are really juvenile!"), they'll be glad to substitute it. One of the flaws of modern slang, of course, is that it's so inexpressive.

At the same time as your child is beginning to flaunt her separation from you, she'll take a greater interest in your conversations, and want to join in. You start to hear "What are you talking about?" more and more. You need to give your child a fairly complete response: "Oh, nothing," or "You wouldn't understand" would be like a slap in the face. Even if it's something as unbearably tedious as insurance, explain. You also start having to be scrupulous about discussing other grown-ups, except in ways that you're willing to share with your child. If your friends the Bensons adopted a puppy from the ASPCA and it turns out that the dog is half St. Bernard, that's a G-rated conversation that she can appropriately overhear and join. The Bensons' business troubles, though, should wait until you have a private moment (some time next year, maybe?).

Your child will want to contribute to conversations, too, and these are no longer the irrelevant interjections of the preschooler. An older child is more likely to take advantage of a pause to launch into a ten-minute lecture on the newly available Inline Skate Barbie.

At moments like this I think longingly of the father in *Cheaper By the Dozen*, who used to roar, "Not of general interest!" when the conversation strayed too far from approved topics. Actually, I think we have to let our children take charge of conversations sometimes, whether or not we are interested in the Triassic-era meat eaters. Even a verbatim recapitulation of the third-grade play is an attempt at adult-style chat. It will get smoother and more refined with time.

School-age children don't need you to do as much *for* them as they used to. But they do want you to do more *with* them, including simply talking. They should already be familiar with the concepts that you don't interrupt, you keep your voice down, you don't call names or make personal remarks, and you say "please" and "thank you" routinely. You'll still be reminding them of all these principles. In addition, it's time to introduce the ones below.

Speak when you're spoken to.

Preschoolers can get away with tongue-tied shyness, but it looks sullen in a child older than seven. If someone says "Hello," your child must say "Hello" back. If someone says, "Do you know what time it is?" She should answer "Yes; it's four-thirty" or "No, I lost my watch last week." If an adult sits her down at the kitchen table and says, "Well, dear, what are you going to be when you grow up?" she can answer "I'm still collecting ideas. What do you do for a living?" or some such thing. Ignoring people is extremely rude and irritating, which is why it works so well on obnoxious younger siblings.

No whispering.

This is a big age for secrets, especially among girls. Don't make the mistake of insisting that the "secret" be pronounced aloud. Chances are your daughter had a good reason for whispering in the first place. But you can remind her that secrets and whispering are rude to everyone who isn't in on the fun. There's a funny story in Betty MacDonald's *Hello, Mrs. Piggle Wiggle* that may discourage the chronic whispering (the whisperer loses her voice temporarily).

You can't really eliminate whispering, but you can hope to limit it until this phase is past.

No muttering.

Whispering is annoying, but sometimes kids do have secrets and need to share them. Muttering, however, is aimed directly at parents. It's often an experiment in insubordination. You tell your daughter to make her bed and she stalks off, saying something under her breath. Chances are she's muttering something she doesn't quite dare say, and if she doesn't dare say it, you probably don't want to hear it. If you're at the boiling point, ignore her. But if you have eight hours of sleep and a good breakfast under your belt, you can say pleasantly, "Honey, don't mutter, I can't understand you." If you're lucky, at this point she'll say, "Oh, nothing" in a huffy tone of voice and you can overlook the whole exchange. If she's spoiling for a fight, she'll tell you what she was mumbling, and then you have to have a confrontation about how much she hates making her bed and how Remy never has to. I don't care where you end up on the bed issue, but make sure your child knows that muttering about her gripes is both rude and ineffective.

Don't be a smart aleck.

Or a smarty-pants, or don't talk back, or whatever. You know what I mean. If the irritating speech of preschoolers is chanting, for grade schoolers it's that heavy-handed sarcasm, taking everything too literally just to prove how smart they are. Mom says, "Come on, quick like a bunny." And the second grader says, "But I'm not a rabbit, Mom." I think children pull this to insert a little distance into the parental relationship. They purposely don't take things the way you mean them, just to establish a thread of independence. This attitude crops up more often when a child is self-conscious or ill at ease. You don't have to like it or applaud it, and you can certainly discourage it when it surfaces. It will vanish, anyway, when your child realizes that he does not, in fact, know everything.

Don't contradict.

Know-it-alls are always right. And they never hesitate to point it out, or tell you just exactly where you're wrong. I have no objection to being corrected, but I want it to be done gently. So I insist on, "No, I don't think so," instead of "Mom, you're wrong." Other substitutes for a flat contradiction are "I read somewhere that . . ." or "José says that . . ." or "But I thought . . ."

Avoid insults.

This is another, more inclusive way of saying "No name-calling." "Duh" seems to be a favorite, as in, "The Sonics are a basketball team, duh. . . ." It's both rude and mean. Even detestable younger siblings don't deserve such treatment.

Say "You're welcome" when someone thanks you.

Our days are full of little exchanges like this that are remarkable only when someone fails to make the correct response. So it's time to start drilling on "You're welcome." Because you're working to teach a new habit, you will have to remind and remind.

When someone says "How are you?" answer "Fine, thanks, how are you?"

Grow-ups take this response for granted, but children don't yet know the words. So if you ask the average eight-year-old how she is, she'll say "Good," or else think hard and say, "Well, I had a headache yesterday but it's gone." You'll need to explain to your child that this is a routine exchange: Someone who wants details will follow up with more questions. Remind her from time to time how it goes—but not around other grown-ups. Better to run through the script ahead of time.

Say "I'm sorry" when you bump into someone.

Or when you step on their toe or otherwise invade their space. Kids operate in a world of their own and often don't recognize when they've disturbed someone. Parents may have to bring this to their attention: "Honey, look, when you bumped the table you spilled my coffee." The normal reaction, of course, is embarrassment, and an embarrassed child is often a tongue-tied child. Which is why you remind kids to say "I'm sorry." If they're equipped with the formula, it's easier for them to rise above a little faux pas.

• C A N   V S.   M A Y •

I'm nearly satisfied if my children makes their requests with the magic word "please" appended. But they really should be saying "May" instead of "Can," as in, "May I use your stapler?" instead of "Can I . . . ?"

Eight or nine is a good time to teach children the distinction, since they're doing so much work on vocabulary at school. "Can" asks about the physical possibility of something. "Can I touch the ceiling?" "May" is a way of asking permission. "May I touch the ceiling?" You may. And if you get on the stepladder, you probably can, too.

The way to teach this distinction to your children is by explaining the difference, and stopping them when they use the words wrong. I sometimes use this as an opportunity to get back at Willy for all of his smart-aleck moments. He'll say, "Mom, can I have some more cereal?" And I'll look at him and say, "I don't know? Can you? Aren't you full yet?" And then he rolls his eyes and says, "May I?" Then Timothy, eager to show off, says "Mommy, may I please have some more cereal?" and looks smugly at his brother and in the ensuing fracas I wonder if I may just go back to bed. Please?

• WHY DON'T YOU HAVE ANY HAIR? •

I tend to make some extravagant claims about the benefits that good manners will bring to you and your children, but one thing I have to be honest about. Even the most polite child will, from time to time, embarrass his parents. The beautiful frankness of childhood ensures this. Kids will ask bald men where their hair went. They will repeat, in astounding detail, that nasty little exchange you had with the bank teller. In drugstores they are drawn to the feminine hygiene shelves with relentless curiosity. And they will pursue taboo subjects with the tenacity of terriers. As a shark can scent blood in water yards away, small children sense embarrassment, and I do believe they enjoy the novelty of watching their parents wriggle with discomfort.

Your children's good manners can't prevent these awful moments. *Your* good manners, though, can cut them short. The first step is to assume an air of detachment. Pretend you're acting a scene in a movie, or pretend you're Mary Poppins, perfectly superior. Then say, "Let's talk about this later," and as soon as you can, remove your child from the scene.

Some kids will be reluctant to change the subject, of course. "Well, why *does* he have a ring through his lip?" they'll ask, even louder than the first query. Your answer should be, "Do you remember what I said about making personal remarks? We'll talk about it later."

Then, even if your child has forgotten the exchange by the time you get to a more private spot, bring the subject up. "Do you remember how you were asking about the ring in that man's lip?" It will be much easier to cut short public inquiries if your child knows that her curiosity *will* be satisfied.

Finally, if your child has clearly offended someone, the simplest and kindest thing you can say is, "I'm sorry."

Play Dates

Intermediate Rules:

Wait to be invited • Going to someone else's house just to use their toys, computer, or video games is not nice • Don't ignore guests (even if they're people your parents stuck you with) • Play with the kid who invited you • Try to cooperate on choosing activities • Don't request special foods or drinks • Report any damage right away, apologize, and offer to help fix it • If you don't want to play with a friend, make a polite excuse

As children begin the elementary school years, they start to take control of their own social lives. Their friendships depend more on common interests or compatible temperaments, less on their mothers' bond or the carpool schedule. And they begin to hatch social schemes under their own steam. All of which is appropriate and quite enjoyable to watch. But some guidance is still important if you want to be sure that your child is always welcome at someone else's house. The rules from Part I still apply, for hosts as well as guests. Hosts greet their guests at the door, offer them the first choice of what to play, take them to the door to say good-bye. Guests follow the rules of the house and thank the host when they're leaving. The children we're happy to see are the ones who have the routine down pat. And there are a few more steps to add when children get a little older.

Wait to be invited.

I am never charmed to hear a high voice on the phone saying, "Can I come over to play?" Chances are that I would actually be happy to have the child here, but it just seems pushy when they invite themselves.

This principle is hard to explain to children, though. In adult terms, the reason you don't invite yourself over is that you don't want to put someone in the uncomfortable position of having to say no. This is too subtle for most kids, but remember, they don't always need to understand your reasoning. You can simply say, "You can't invite yourself over to Martha's house because that's rude. Why don't we see if she can come here instead?" And then sometimes when you call to make these arrangements, the parent or baby-sitter will say, "Martha's been over at your house a lot lately, why don't you bring Sophie over here?" So everybody gets what they want, in an extremely polite way.

Of course some lucky children live in neighborhoods where they can wander from house to house. Older children also take more initiative in arranging their own social lives, and are more likely simply to announce, "Mom, I'm going over to Jesse's house." At that point you assume Jesse checked with his mother before inviting your son over. It's only when parents are closely involved in play-time planning that you have to enforce this ban on self-invitation.

Going to someone else's house just to use their toys, computer, or video games is not nice.

Since you have no idea what your child does at someone else's house, you may need to investigate a little to find out if she's guilty of this. "What did you do with Lucy? Oh, did she *want* to play on the computer for the whole afternoon? Well, honey, how do you think that makes her feel? She probably thinks you like the computer better than her." Now, children being what they are, your daughter may very well admit that the only thing she likes about Lucy is Lucy's Macintosh, with the "World of Barbie" CD-ROM. If you feel this is really true, you'll be doing Lucy a kindness and teaching your daughter a lesson if you limit their play for a while. On the other hand, you may have a play date at your house when you notice that your son is sitting disconsolate on the living room sofa, leafing through a book, while his playmate steers Sonic the Hedgehog through the pits of bubbling lava. It's a painful situation to witness, but it can be useful. When the guest is gone you can discuss how it made your child feel to be ignored in favor of his toys. Any child this has happened to is unlikely to forget it.

Don't ignore guests (even if they're people your parents stuck you with).

We had some friends over recently and the social synergy between their children and ours was disastrous. Will sat reading while Molly stared into space until my husband jumped in and got them started on a game of Clue. Usually this kind of frozen incompatibility needs some help from the adults, but you can also prime your child in advance. "The Davises are coming for lunch with their children. Can you think of some things you might be able to do with Jordan?" Board games and puzzles are a real godsend in this situation and you might even consider keeping a new puzzle in a closet for such an occasion.

Kids may not understand their responsibility to entertain their guests, even the ones they've chosen and invited themselves. You may have to point out that it's rude to reorganize Barbie's wardrobe unless that's what a guest wants to do. A play date is also not the time to chat on the phone. Your child can answer a quick question about homework, but otherwise he should say, "I'm sorry, Jake, we have company so I can't talk right now." Usually a couple of pointers from you will set your child straight.

Play with the kid who invited you.

Or play with the kid you invited. Grown-ups say you should "dance with the one who brought you." In other words, say Sabrina invites Lydia to go to the beach. When they're there, Lydia runs into her friend Frances, whom she knows from ballet. It's fine for the three to join forces to build an incredible lagoon, but Lydia should not go running off with Frances, leaving Sabrina looking sadly out at the waves. Kids are quick to empathize about social

rejection, so a few quiet words from you will help your child understand that it's important to stick with the friend with whom she
originally made plans. (See "The Better Invitation Club," page 102).
And although threesomes are usually awkward with preschoolers,
a trio of older kids who know each other well usually gets along
just fine. As long as the original pairing is part of the mix, including
a third child is a good option.

Try to cooperate on choosing activities.

We've all had disastrous occasions when children were tired or
had new toys they didn't feel like sharing or were right in the middle
of an engrossing project or fantasy and couldn't fit another child
into it. This situation, like the one above, often requires adult inter-
vention, and sometimes play dates need to be cut short if they aren't
taking off. But as a rule, children should try to compromise on
finding something to do. Playgrounds are full of methods for handling this situation: Kids can take turns choosing the activity, they
can toss coins, they can do "Eenie Meenie Miney Moe." You may
need to remind your child of this only occasionally, because it's a
principle her playmates will enforce.

Don't request special foods or drinks.

I don't think I've ever had children at my house for more than
an hour without feeding them. Even if a parent doesn't offer a snack,
I think it's perfectly all right for a child of eight or nine to say, "Mrs.
Kent, I'm awfully hungry. Could I please have a snack?" But if I
offer a choice of two or three foods and the child says, "What else
do you have?" or "Do you have any corn chips?" my smile fades a
little. And I start to think huffy thoughts like, "I'm not running a
restaurant here!" A child may choose from among the foods or
drinks offered, but can't ask to have the selection broadened. You'll
have to tell your child this, and trust that she remembers when she's
a guest, since you aren't around to remind her.

Report any damage right away, apologize, and offer to help fix it.

You know what I mean: balls through windows, bottles of nail polish spilled on the quilt, floppy disks stuck in the disk drive. Grown-ups can sometimes fix disasters if they find out about them soon enough. In any case, a heartfelt apology is always crucial. As you're explaining this principle to your own child, try to remember (or make up) a similar case from your own childhood to illustrate the point that everybody makes mistakes. Like the time when you flushed Mrs. Johnson's toilet and the handle came off in your hand and you were so embarrassed that you hid it in a flowerpot and Mrs. Johnson saw you and you wanted to die. Or whatever.

If you don't want to play with a friend, make a polite excuse.

Face it, turning down an invitation is rejection. So we have to help our children phrase it as softly as possible. (See "The Social Fib," below) "I'm sorry, we have family plans," is a great all-purpose excuse. You could also suggest that your child say, "I need to check with my parents, may I call you back?" This will give the two of you breathing space to come up with a gentle way out of the invitation.

As they get older, children start building relationships with adults independently of you. Most of these adults will be the parents of their friends, and if your child follows the rules above, he'll always be a welcome and popular guest.

• THE SOCIAL FIB •

Honesty is the best policy in most areas of life, but good manners sometimes require a little bit of deception. Since we want our children to be truthful, you may hesitate to teach your offspring this facet of politeness. But you should, because the underlying motive for social fibs is empathy. These are the lies you tell when the truth would hurt someone's feelings.

For instance, we live near the George Washington Bridge, and there is a well-known children's book about the bridge called *The Little Red Lighthouse and the Great Gray Bridge*. We must have received five copies of this book since the children were born. When the third one arrived, Willy, then five, tore off the wrapping and gravely said, "Oh, this is one of my favorite books."

Well, it's not. But bless his heart, he somehow knew that this would be a kinder remark than, "We already have two of these."

Children grasp the principle of the social fib with surprising ease, especially if they're naturally empathetic or if you've been working on "How would you feel if. . . ." questions. They are certainly familiar with the idea of hurting someone's feelings. So let them see you massaging the truth to spare someone's feelings. Say a friend calls your son for a play date. He can't go because he's going to a birthday party, to which the friend was not invited. So you say, "We'll tell Christopher you're doing something with the family, because he wasn't invited to Kareem's party and that might hurt his feelings." And when you think your child is capable of a little kind-hearted invention, you can turn it over to her. "Marisa wants you to sleep over at her house, but I know you don't really like her. How do you think you can say no nicely?"

There aren't that many situations that call for a social fib: the unwanted gift, the excluded friend, the unwelcome invitation, and the unenjoyable experience. Parties that aren't fun. Movies that are boring. Weird food. When I was about twelve, a friend of mine had a sleepover birthday party. Her mother, who was an early advocate of natural foods, had gone to great trouble and compromised her ideals to bake a birthday cake from a Betty Crocker mix. There was clearly something wrong with the cake: It was only about an inch thick, even with two layers. We all behaved beautifully; accepting the flat little slices and taking a few careful bites. Some brave soul even said, "It's very good."

That's a magnificent example of a social fib. It's not the kind of deception you have to cover up, because if the truth is found out (or if it's staring everyone in the face), the teller of the untruth only looks kind and well-intentioned. Which indeed she is.

Telephone Manners

Intermediate Rules:

Speak clearly • Say "Just a minute, please" • Don't drop the receiver • Don't shout • Tolerate small talk • Take a message if the grown-ups aren't available • Identify yourself • Greet whoever answers the phone, if you know them • Ask politely for your friend • Say "Thank you" • Ask to leave a message • Say "Good-bye" before hanging up • Apologize for wrong numbers • Leave a short message on the answering machine

Using the telephone seems like a real privilege to many school-age children; it's a mark of maturity and competence. But the telephone is also an interface between the household and the outside world, so you need to make sure your children do a good job of representing you. What's more, you need to lay good groundwork now for the years just ahead, when older kids start to view the telephone as a lifeline.

Unfortunately, safety plays a part here, too. Children should never tell a caller that they're at home alone. Some safety experts warn that children should not give their names when they answer the phone, because a caller could use that information to gain their confidence. Manners take a backseat to safety, of course, so be sure your child knows that he should hang up instantly if a telephone call makes him uneasy. If the phone rings again right away, he should get an adult to answer it or just let it ring.

In Part I, I discussed some basic rules for using the telephone, like saying "Please" and speaking slowly and not listening to other people's calls on an extension. They're worth reviewing if you think your child might sound a little gruff on the phone.

On the other hand, if she's pretty smooth, she may want to take over phone-answering chores entirely. This can be helpful, if you can trust her to observe the following conventions. These skills are easier to teach than table manners because kids really want to get them right. You won't have to nag much: Just issue a few reminders from time to time, or run a quick review of these rules.

Speak clearly.

Many adults find it a little unnerving when a child answers the phone, and it makes everyone uncomfortable if your child has to repeat everything he says. Some kids have speech patterns (a lisp, for instance) that make them hard to understand. That doesn't mean they can't answer the phone. Just give them something to say that doesn't involve that difficulty. ("Klein house" instead of "Hello, Thally thpeaking.")

Say "Just a minute, please."

If the call is not for the child answering the phone, he should courteously ask the caller to wait, instead of just vanishing and leaving dead air.

Don't drop the receiver.

Yes, you probably do have to spell this out to your child, or she won't know that the clatter will echo in the caller's head for several minutes.

Don't shout.

"Mom, it's for you!" bellowed next to the receiver is perfectly natural behavior for a child, but not kind to an adult caller. The child should put the receiver down gently and, ideally, walk to the room where he'll find the person the call is for. I do understand how rare this behavior is, but there's nothing wrong with aiming high. Or with hissing, as you hurry toward the telephone, "Honey, I wish you could remember to come get me instead of shouting."

Tolerate small talk.

Most children of early school age have a utilitarian view of the phone. The notion of using it to chat hasn't emerged yet, so you often hear a note of puzzlement in an eight-year-old's voice when you say, "How's school?" and she answers, "Fine." She's thinking, "Why is this person asking me that?" As a parent, you may need to explain that people who know her sometimes like to talk a little bit on the phone. I don't know many kids this age who can work up enthusiasm about the custom, but we have this convention in our society that you don't say bluntly, "What are you calling for? Whaddya want?"

Take a message if the grown-ups aren't available.

Make this as easy for your child as possible. Keep paper and pencil by every phone. (Some kids may be entertained by those pink message pads used in offices, with all the boxes to check.) You can help by asking "Did anyone call?" when you come home. It will also encourage your child if you take messages for her in an efficient manner.

By the time your children are seven, you can't stand over them any more, feeding them cues for their phone conversations. They wouldn't stand for it. But you should make sure that when your child picks up the phone to check a homework assignment or arrange a sleepover, she follows these rules. If you happen to overhear her missing a few of these steps, remind her when the call is over, "Honey, it's nicer if you. . . ."

Identify yourself.

When a child places a phone call she should say, "Hello, this is Susanna."

Greet whoever answers the phone, if you know them.

My second grader has an extremely suave friend who is ready to set up as a telephone salesman right now. "Hi, Carol? This is David. How was your vacation? Did you guys have a good time in California?" Nothing flatters a parent more than being treated as a *person* by one of their children's friends.

Ask politely for your friend.

Not "I want to talk to Alex" which sounds like a demand, but "Could I please speak to Alex?"

Say "Thank you."

After all, Alex's mother is not Alex's secretary.

Ask to leave a message.

"Oh. Okay," followed by the phone being hung up is awfully abrupt. You need to coach your child in the polite formulas, which are, "Could you please have him call me?" or "May I leave a message, please?" or even, "Okay. Thank you."

Say "Good-bye" before hanging up.

Apologize for wrong numbers.

This is worth rehearsing, because it can throw a child into a panic. When she gets a wrong number, she should just say, "I'm sorry," and hang up. The apology is important, though.

Leave a short message on the answering machine.

Just like adults, children vary in their comfort level with answering machines. If she's poised enough to say, "This is Caroline, calling for Teresa," that's fine. But if the answering machine makes her nervous, she should hang up rather than leave a garbled mumble on the tape.

When these rules become habit in your house, you'll know that your child can enter the phone-mania of the preteen years with perfect politeness.

In the Car

A polite greeting is essential • Punctuality counts •
Changes in schedule must be shared with the driver
• Belongings should go with the correct passenger
• Passengers should thank the chauffeur

As children get older, they start spending more and more time in other people's cars. It's pretty easy for a car-pool driver to figure out what kind of behavior she'd like to see from her juvenile passengers. That's the kind of behavior you want to teach your kids. But just in case you haven't set foot in a minivan for a while, here are some suggestions. Since the very notion of "carpool" suggests that you won't always be present, extracting these courtesies from your riders in a very obvious way is probably the best way to teach them to your own children.

A polite greeting is essential.

"Hi, Mrs. Green" is good enough. It's just that most parents don't like to be considered an inanimate but convenient option provided by Ford, like an oversize cupholder with a voice. Of course the best way to elicit a greeting is to proffer one yourself.

Punctuality counts.

When I was a child, there was one car-pool mother who never waited. She was always on time (if not early) and if we weren't at the end of the driveway by the time her station wagon pulled up, she'd drive off. She'd even drive away if she could see us pelting toward the street, book bags banging our legs. Of course she took things a little far, but I can see how she'd get impatient. You can expostulate gently with kids who consistently keep you waiting. You can also point out to your own child how frustrating you find this, to hammer home the point that frequently being late is really rude. Naturally you have to respect other people's schedules, too, to set a good example.

Changes in schedule must be shared with the driver.

There's nothing more infuriating than waiting for twenty minutes with a car full of kids for a child who left school early for an orthodontist's appointment. Notifying a driver of changes in routine is really a parent's job, but kids should know how important it is so they can start taking on some of the responsibility.

Belongings should go with the correct passenger.

You can't do your homework if your backpack is in Mr. Levy's car, can you? And it's not Mr. Levy's job to get back in his car and deliver the backpack you forgot. Difficult as it is for children to keep track of their possessions, they must learn. If your child frequently leaves things behind, let her take the rap. The homework stays undone, or she has to go through ballet class in her jeans. It's hard, but it's a lesson she won't forget.

Passenger should thank the chauffeur.

Nothing annoys me more than being taken for granted by somebody else's child. Often I have to say, in a prompting tone of voice, "You're welcome, Sarah . . ." That usually gets them. I'm sure they think I'm a witch but I'd rather be a witch than a cup-holder. "Goodbye, thanks!" is all I need to hear.

Party Manners

Greet the adult host • Be a good sport • Don't complain • Thank whoever gives you the party bag • Thank the party child and adult host when you leave • *Extra Credit: Tell the hosts you had a good time

I've noticed that as children get older, a veneer of civilization settles over even the wildest among them. By the age of six or so, most kids can do a pretty good imitation of a calm, law-abiding individual, and keep it up for as long as an hour. Unless they're under a lot of pressure. Attending your own birthday party may be the most thrilling day of the year, but it's still stressful, and right through second grade (or third, for the sensitive), Birthday Kid Meltdown is a common phenomenon. Everybody tactfully ignores it, and the tears or fury are left out of the official version of the birthday memory.

But while we still extend considerable tolerance to birthday kids, the emotional free-for-all of the preschool party should calm down considerably. School-age kids, who've been to lots of parties by the time they hit first grade, should be able to manage the activities with aplomb. They should also be able to manage the courtesies listed here.

Since parents rarely stay at parties with their children after the age of six or so, you may want to run through this list before dropping your child off with his present. Some of these behaviors should be automatic, but some are specific to the occasion. To be honest, the harassed parent/hosts probably won't notice if some of these forms of politeness are overlooked. But if your child *does* produce them, she's sure to make a terrific impression.

Greet the adult host.

It's natural enough for a child to seek out the party girl and hand over the present. But it's also important to say a pleasant "Hello" to the adult who's giving the party. Most grown-ups will make this easy by taking the initiative and greeting their guests. All a child really has to say is, "Hi, Ms. Farley." And maybe add a smile.

Be a good sport.

When we were growing up, party games were always competitive, and only a handful of kids got prizes. Nowadays parents often devise cooperative games to avoid increasing tension. But kids love to compete. And where there are winners, there are also losers. The rules of good sportsmanship (see page 115) still hold at a party.

Don't complain.

Giving a birthday party for a child is not fun. There's too much to think about and the noise level is unbearably high. Complaints are completely out of place. This year at Will's birthday party, the guests played football and baseball, except for one boy, who didn't like either sport. So he kicked a soccer ball around aimlessly until everybody came inside for the cake. I felt sorry for him, but I was too busy to do anything about entertaining him. And I certainly appreciated his stoic endurance of an experience that clearly wasn't enjoyable for him. I thought that was really polite.

Thank whoever gives you the party bag.

Party bags are another terrible burden on parents. i think we'd probably all love to abolish them, but we don't know how to get organized to do it. In the meantime, kids expect them. Just watch their eyes as they enter the room, trying to scope out where the favors have been stashed. They should thank whoever hands them the goodies, even though they do feel entitled.

Thank the party child and adult host when you leave.

If you pick up your own child from the party you can prompt a grateful good-bye. If you won't be there to nag, feel free to remind your child before the party. I'm not saying it's going to work, but you will have made an effort.

*Extra Credit: Tell the hosts you had a good time.

This may be an example of a social lie. Or maybe it's just good manners copying genuine enthusiasm. Even if your child is a terrible actor and can't disguise the fact that he really didn't like the 3-D movie, putting a pleasant face on things will endear him to the grown-ups. Now and in the future.

• THE BETTER INVITATION CLUB •

Do you remember this from your childhood? You are scheduled to spend the night at Susie's house, and Linda, the glamorous new girl in class, invites you over to her house. You desperately want to go to Linda's instead of to Susie's. But your mom insists you go to boring old Susie's as you had planned. Maybe she even used the old-fashioned formula: "We're not members of the Better Invitation Club."

Well, Mom was right, as of course you perceive now. It's cruel to discard plans with one friend because something more attractive comes up. And sooner or later, the issue will arise with your children. Be prepared for it with a firm family policy: You do what you were first invited to do.

"But what if?" you'll be thinking. "What if Leonora gets invited to go skiing for the weekend?" "What if André's grandparents come to town unexpectedly?" "What if Dad gets tickets to a Pacers game?" Of course there are exceptions. If the second, conflicting invitation is for something really special, a one-time offer, then it's fair to consider it. And this is a case where parents can step in to manage their child's social life. Because it's such a delicate situation, with so much potential for hurt feelings, the parent of the child with conflicting invitations should call the mother or father of the other child and explain. "I know Mary was supposed to sleep over with Samantha this Friday, but her father didn't know that and he bought seats for the *Nutcracker.*" Then you attempt to make amends. "I know Sammy will be disappointed: Do you think she could come over here on Saturday?" Try to make a firm rain date, indicating that the friendship is still important to your child.

Under no circumstances should you or your child lie to get out of an invitation that's been accepted. It sets a bad example for your kids and it's too easy to get caught. The hallmark of an acceptable social lie (also known as "The Social Fib") is that nobody will look worse if it gets found out. This kind of lie doesn't pass that test.

Chances are that you will occasionally be on the receiving end of this situation, and then the gracious move is to release your child's friend from the original commitment. "Of course Tabitha should go to the rodeo. Let's see if we can reschedule her dinner here." If you suspect your child is actually being relegated to second-best, just be even *more* polite. "Frank is going to Barney's for dinner that night instead of coming here? How nice. Peter will be very disappointed." At this point a lively sense of empathy will tell you that that other parent feels just terrible. And so she should.

Thank-You Notes

Two or three sentences are plenty • Mistakes are okay • Use special stationery • Using the computer is fine if you personalize the letter • Parents write addresses • Notes should be sent within a week of receiving a gift

When children are very small, you write thank-you notes for them or with them. You hope that they'll grasp the idea of expressing gratitude, but the most important part of the project is letting someone know how grateful *you* are for their warmth toward your child. And let's face it, most of the effort is frankly yours.

The balance should shift, though, once your children can write. Of course you still want to communicate gratitude. But you also insist that they write thank-you notes so that they learn how to do it. Writing thank-you notes is a habit, just like saying "please."

Not that your child has to write a note for every gift he receives at his birthday party. You may remember from Part I that notes must be written to special grown-ups, for special treats, and for presents not opened in the presence of the donor. I think this is a good rule of thumb throughout childhood. For a child to write a civil note takes a lot of effort, and I don't think most kids really get excited by a thank-you note from their peers. Unlike adults, who do (or who get excited in the wrong way by the absence of same). What's more, you don't want to overburden your child and make this note-writing into a horrible big issue so that she'll never produce another letter in her life, even when she gets married. You still need to keep things as simple as possible.

If your child doesn't open his presents at a birthday party, though, I think it is important that the gifts be acknowledged. This can be a big job, so you might want to help out a little more, perhaps by photocopying a basic letter and leaving blanks for your child to fill in: "Dear . . . Thanks for the. . . . I will enjoy using it for. . . ." I wouldn't generally recommend this tactic, but if you don't cheat a little, your child may be overwhelmed by the chore. And her pals won't care one way or the other.

Children's ability to write varies enormously at this age. Gripping a pencil and forming letters is a very complex skill. When you add concerns like spelling and punctuation, content is bound to get shoved aside. This is fine. My husband, Rick, once told me a story about an African tribesman presenting an American visitor with a seashell for Christmas. The American exclaimed, "But we're so far from the beach!" And the tribesman answered, "Long walk is part of gift." The story seems too pat to be true, but the punch line has entered our family language. There are times when the effort involved in an action counts for a great deal. I feel that way about thank-you notes from first- and second-graders. The anxiety and straggly lines and stiff language are part of the message. Given the arduousness of the task, here are some suggestions to make it easier.

Two or three sentences are plenty.

Try to make sure your child keeps notes short so she doesn't burn out. Willy tends to start out writing a long, involved epistle, and then he runs out of steam halfway through. "Dear Gran, Thank you for the new mitt. I can't wait for baseball to start. Love, Yvette," is a perfect note from a child this age.

Mistakes are okay.

You won't really be able to convince a perfectionist of this, but you can try. Don't hover and point out errors. You can glance over the note when it's done in an admiring way, praising the neatness or the way the date is written or *something.* Your goal at this point is to make the task as easy and pleasant as possible.

Use special stationery.

You wouldn't write a thank-you note on the paper you use for a shopping list. Your child should write notes on something a little more festive, too. Construction paper is all right, especially if she takes the time to decorate it. Or printed letter paper works well, too: A couple of cowboys doing a jig at the bottom of a page dresses up the message. It also takes up space, which can be important. Sometimes kids think they need to write enough to fill the page. No wonder they feel overwhelmed by the task! You might want to provide new markers or let your child use one of your favorite fine-point pens to sweeten the deal.

Using the computer is fine if you personalize the letter.

In other words, thank-you notes mustn't look like form letters. You could make a template with a border and fancy type, just changing the name of the correspondent and the gift. But be sure that human hands touch the page somehow, either by signing or coloring or decorating with stickers. This is particularly important when writing notes to older adults, who believe personal correspondence should be hand-written.

Parents write addresses.

Unless your child is having a great time turning out these notes, you can lighten the burden by doing the secretarial work: addressing envelopes, putting on the stamps, etc. When you begin to feel that you're doing a job your child could do perfectly well herself, you can hand it over to her.

Notes should be sent within a week of receiving a gift.

This may be a goal rather than a rule. But promptness is a great virtue in this field, and it's also a lot easier to motivate a child to write a note while a gift is still new or the memory of an experience is fresh. And you will have to provide the motivation: No child is going to finish her homework and think to herself, What shall I do now? I know: I'll write thank-you notes!

The bonus is that you can anticipate some reflected glory. I know that my goddaughter in Kansas City wouldn't have thought, all by herself, of thanking me for the bead kit I sent her. But I love knowing from her note that she used some of the beads on her Halloween costume. This strengthens my bond to her, and it makes me think that her mother is doing a very good job of bringing her up. Just think: This kind of appreciation can be yours the next time those notes get in the mail.

• GETTING AND GIVING PRESENTS •

Nobody expects a particularly coherent or polite response from a four-year-old opening a present. What you see is the honest reaction, whether it's bliss or puzzlement or indifference. When children get older, though, our expectations change. I know that the freshness and honesty of children are delightful, but if you have just given your six-year-old godson a hand-knitted sweater with a rabbit on it that you nearly lost your eyesight over, a little enthusiasm is called for.

If a child is genuinely pleased with a gift, his pleasure cannot be hidden. The big grin and the glowing eyes are completely eloquent. Still, everyone who gives a child a gift should be thanked. If a child needs to be prompted, it's more tactful for a parent to sidle over and whisper the prompt in the ear rather than bellow across the room, "What do you say, Hannah?" (If the giver isn't present or if the gift is especially lavish, a thank-you note is called for.)

If a child isn't thrilled by the gift, a polite response is still necessary. This requires some planning and maybe even role-playing. Three weeks before you go to Grandma's for Christmas, you might point out that sometimes she gives funny gifts. (Be careful about your tone, though: Always stress the effort and thoughtfulness that went into choosing any gift.) What do your children say? They say thank you, and if possible add a sentence of praise.

You can act this out at home by handing your child something really odd, and together coming up with a suitable enthusiastic phrase. One year at Christmas I opened a present from an aunt. As I tore off the wrapping paper, I saw that the box said General Electric Steam Iron. I remember taking a deep breath and saying "Oh, wow, an iron!" meanwhile thinking, "I'm eleven, what am I going to do with an iron?" Imagine my relief when the box turned out to be full of pecans. At least I could eat them.

Trying to please the recipient is the basic dynamic of gift-giving, and it should also rule your child's choices of gifts. By the time a child is six or so, she can understand that what she gives Elsie is not necessarily what she wants herself, but what she thinks Elsie might enjoy. In other words, Elsie adores horses, so you give her a new horse book instead of the Barbie that your daughter might prefer.

When a child gives a present to someone else, child or adult, he sets it gently in the recipient's hands and says, "Happy Birthday" or "Merry Christmas" or whatever. He may say, "I hope you like my present," but he doesn't say what it is or how much it cost. And then, the hardest point of all, he lets go of it.

Good Housemates

When our children are very small, we have to do everything for them. When they get older and more capable, we try to get them to do things for themselves, but sometimes it's just easier to take over and throw the dirty socks into the laundry basket instead of telling your child six times to do it.

And yet there are manners involved in sharing a house with people, as anyone who has ever had a roommate can attest. Did you like that girl who always ate the last yogurt in the refrigerator? Or what about the guy who always took the newspaper to work before anyone else saw it, and never brought it back? There are people in this world who are plumb selfish and will do what they want, knowing how much it will annoy everyone. (We assume that our children will not be such monsters.) There are also people in the world who have simply never been trained in the courteous sharing of a dwelling place. You don't want your child to belong to this group, do you? School-age children should be capable of meeting these requirements:

Pick up what you leave around the house.

Children don't know, without being told, how annoying it is to have their toys lying all over the place. Or to leave their homework on the kitchen table when it's finished. Putting away what you're finished with is not, I guess, a natural impulse. So you need to introduce the idea to children, and then remind them when they forget. "Honey, would you put away the Monopoly board, please?" Over and over again.

Put the cap back on the toothpaste tube.

Marriages have broken up over uncapped toothpaste tubes, but a child of five has the dexterity to replace the darn thing. Remind your child that it's as much part of brushing his teeth as spitting. When you begin to suspect he's not hearing you any more, try letting the toothpaste dry out, capless, for a couple of days (after securing your own alternative supply, of course).

Rinse the toothpaste out of the sink after brushing your teeth.

I know this sounds petty, but when you share the sink with someone who uses sparkle gel toothpaste, it becomes a pretty big factor in domestic peace. Show your child how to splash away those toothpaste streaks with a squirt of water from her mouth, or while she's rinsing off her toothbrush. Check the sink after she's brushed. Remind and remind. All right—nag.

Clean the dirt off the soap.

Yes, clean the soap. When a kid with filthy hands washes them, some of the grime ends up on that cake of Ivory. A quick swish under the running water gets rid of it, but no child will bother to swish it unless you insist. And insist again.

Put down the toilet seat when you're done.

(This is applicable only in households with males.) This should be an automatic gesture, like locking the door when you leave the house. It's a habit that you have to instill with reminders. Because we all become blind and deaf to our surroundings, change the medium of your nagging from time to time. Try putting a sign behind the toilet. When you think it's become invisible, Write "Put me down!" on a piece of masking tape and stick it onto the underside of the toilet seat. It's worth all the trouble: This is an issue on which your son's future girlfriends will judge you sternly.

Put your dirty clothes in the laundry hamper.

Is this discipline or manners? I think it's courtesy to the person who is going to be doing the laundry, not to mention courtesy to a sibling who may share one's room. Again, a combination of prompting and consequences should get this message across. You remind your child where those clothes should go. And inform her that any clothes that she didn't put into the hamper aren't going to be washed. The first time she reaches for her tie-dyed leggings and they aren't in her bureau will be unpleasant, but it will also make your point.

Put your dishes in the dishwasher.

Unless you're afraid the Limoges will get chipped, you can trust a seven-year-old to put a plate, a bowl, a cup, and a fork into the dishwasher. You may have to reload them, or even take them out and rinse them, but it's worth the effort. Show your child how you want it to be done: Plates go here, bowls go here. And when she asks to be excused from the table (remember, she's supposed to ask), you say, "Yes, you may, and would you put your plate in the dishwasher please?" Eventually you will be able to leave off the request, and the plate will find its way to the dishwasher automatically.

Clean up after spills.

When children spill their juice at Timo's preschool, they get up from the table and grab a sponge from the sink and mop it up. So why can't I get the kids to do this at home? Probably because I'm too quick to leap in myself, sponge at the ready. When I'm not on automatic pilot, though, I hang back and say, "Okay, get the sponge, sweetie, and wipe it up," when the milk hits the floor. It's important for children to understand that the desirable reaction to a minor mishap like a spill is not helplessness. (I also think it's probably good for kids to know they're capable of cleaning up their own messes.) The difficult part about teaching this habit is hard for parents, not kids. Don't do it yourself, just hand over the paper towels.

If a door is closed, knock before you go in.

A few days ago I wanted to get my hairbrush out of the bathroom. The door was closed, so I knocked and waited. There was no answer, so I pushed the door open. And Willy roared from inside, "Timo! Get out!" I backed out in a hurry and realized that I hadn't ever explained to the boys about knocking on doors and saying, "Come in" or "I'll be right out." It was a crystal clear illustration of the fact that, where manners are concerned, you just have to tell children what the system is. They cannot figure it out for themselves. Of course an eager child will not remember to knock, and you'll have to remind her over and over again. Some adults never remember either.

The rules in this section are simple and they may seem small-minded. But kids have to learn how to be good roommates, and before you know it, your reminders will pay off. You won't hesitate to enter the bathroom, and you may even be able to walk through your house without tripping over a roller skate and a pair of Barbie dolls.

• THE SHOUTING GAME •

When I was growing up my mother used to have a fit about something I couldn't understand: She hated to have us shouting from room to room. At one point she got so worked up about it that we took to using the phone to call the kitchen from an upstairs bedroom. (We were much too lazy to go downstairs, of course.)

This is another one of those puzzles that has been solved with time. I now live in a two-bedroom apartment, but my children still tend to shout for me. "Mom!" comes the summons.

I used to answer. To be honest, I used to come running, as I had when they were infants and got stuck in the closet because they only knew how to crawl backward. But now they're big boys and if they want me to sign a spelling test or find the top for the pink marker, they can come find me and tell me so, in civilized voices.

So now I don't answer. I pretend there's water running so that I can't hear the summons. (Sometimes I have to grit my teeth so I won't shout back something like "Stop shouting!") Eventually, they come trotting to where I am. Unless, in a moment of weakness, I break down first and go find out what they want, undermining the whole exchange.

• IN SICKNESS AND IN HEALTH •

Every now and then my children, who have been rampaging around the apartment until dinner is set on the table, suddenly fall ill. Their heads ache. Their stomachs ache. Their throats hurt. They feel as if they need to throw up. They groan and grimace and act out all these symptoms with a panache that would reach a near-sighted viewer hundreds of yards away.

Hard-hearted mother that I am, I tend to ignore them. I'm even ignoring what might be the underlying cause of this sudden ill health (distaste for my cooking?). I don't believe people should suffer in silence, but melodramatic complaints don't have anything to do with good manners. Especially when the aches and pains are induced by nothing worse than the threat of dinner. Even genuine ill health has its protocol.

No faking.

The story of the boy who cried wolf can be trotted out there. If you pretend to be sick when you aren't, nobody will believe you when you really need sympathy or grape-flavored children's Tylenol.

Keep complaints to a minimum.

It's important to let the grown-ups in charge know how you feel. But beyond the informative discussion of symptoms, further moaning and groaning actually inhibit sympathy. Self-control is not usually a quality children possess in abundance, though.

I am not actually hard-hearted, and if a child is in real discomfort, he or she deserves plenty of TLC. But dwelling on aches and pains has a way of prolonging them. What's more—and you can try explaining this to an older child—a patient who doesn't complain often gets more sympathy than one who does. Ask any nurse.

Blow your nose with tissues, then throw the tissues away.

I have no success with this; my children snuffle like pug dogs. But I have seen and admired other children who grab a handful of tissues, give a big honk, and dispose of the result.

Cover your mouth when you cough or sneeze.

Do the latest medical findings uphold this technique as a method of inhibiting the spread of germs? Who cares; it's traditional. And washing hands afterward adds a level of effectiveness to the disease-prevention theory.

Say "God bless you!" when someone sneezes.

This is one of the strangest little cultural leftovers we have. Back in the Middle Ages, people believed that when you sneezed, your soul left your body for a moment. So the people around said "God bless you" as a way of protecting the soul during its momentary exposure to the world. (The German habit of saying "Gesundheit!" or "Health!" makes a little more sense.) It's not logical, but the practice hangs on to the extent that friendly strangers often say it when someone sneezes in a crowd. The sneezer then says, "Thank you." It may be easiest to teach this habit when children are very young and still fascinated by the funny things your body does all by itself.

Good Sportsmanship

Intermediate Rules:

Follow the rules • Don't rejoice too much when you win • Don't fuss when you lose • *Extra credit: Compliment your opponent

Competition is a huge part of childhood, and it really heats up in the school years. Kids need to measure themselves against their friends; it's their way of finding out who they are. "I'm not as fast a runner as Jing, but I can beat her at chess every time." Or, "Kevin is the best in the class at math, but he doesn't spell very well." So winning and losing matters enormously. It's sometimes a child's total measure of himself—for that day, at least. What's more, children don't have an adult sense of proportion. They don't know that losing a soccer game in kindergarten *doesn't* mean you're going to be a loser for the rest of your life.

As children mature, though, they acquire enough experience to be able to put various wins and losses in perspective. A boy in his fifth Little League season knows that he may strike out once and manage a solid base hit the next time he comes up to bat. Or that he might win the spelling bee this week and be taken out in the second round next week.

Because they have this sense of perspective, it's easier for older children to be good sports. But younger kids need to be introduced to the elements of sportsmanship, too. They may find these rules hard to follow at first, but this is an area of manners that peers police very carefully. As a parent you can describe the right behavior, and reinforce it when it occurs. But you don't have to do much else. Your child's friends will provide all the necessary reminders.

Follow the rules.

Every competition has its rules, some of them quite complex. A child who doesn't follow the rules—or tries to change them in the middle of the game—won't be allowed to play for very long. The "level playing field" was surely invented by kids, who won't tolerate anything they perceive as unfair. You won't have to remind your child of this principle, but you might suggest that, when he joins a new group of kids, he ask about the rules of the game before starting to play.

Don't rejoice too much when you win.

Winning feels great, and nobody can help smiling or even grinning at a victory. But prancing around, pumping the air, and showing everybody the A on a book report will not make any friends. If you catch your child in this kind of behavior, draw her aside and point out quietly that she's probably making everybody else feel terrible. If your family watches sports on TV, you see a lot of this kind of strutting. Comment on it and let your child know how much you disapprove.

Don't fuss when you lose.

I'm a great figure-skating fan and I made Tonya Harding an object lesson for my children. Unlike Tonya, I told them, good competitors enter the arena, do their best, and don't pitch a hissy fit when things don't go the way they'd planned. This is probably the most difficult lesson for small children to absorb, but self-control along with peer pressure will eventually do the job (for most people, anyway). You don't want to stifle your child, of course. Disappointment is completely legitimate. But there's a huge gap between a glum, disappointed face and a tantrum, which would be totally unacceptable.

*Extra credit: compliment your opponent.

Every now and then, reading the sports pages, I come across generous remarks made by competitors about their opponents. "She just ran a beautiful race today," or "His service return was phenomenal." I wouldn't expect a child to be this generous or this analytical. But you can teach a six-year-old to say, "Nice game," at the end of a hand of Go Fish. And you can point out how well she played. And if merely modeling good behavior isn't enough, when she's a bit older you can suggest that she find something specific to comment on. Maybe her opponent had great luck or her skill has improved. Nobody really expects this level of gracious conduct, which is why I call it "extra credit." But if your child can lose to you at Monopoly and say, "You were really smart to buy all the railroads," you'll know she's a really good sport.

Entertaining Grown-Ups

Intermediate Rules:

Greet adult guests • Submit to small talk • Surrender
the living room to the adults • Help out as hosts • Try
not to interrupt grow-up conversation • Say "Good
night" to the guests • Stay in bed

When I was a little girl my parents had frequent dinner parties. We never ate with the grown-ups, but we did have to put in an appearance. We passed hors d'oeuvres, and we always had to come in to say "Good night," going around the circle of adults shaking hands or enduring kisses.

I don't live or entertain the way my parents did, but we do often have friends over for dinner, and since we live in a small apartment, the boys are right there, under foot. We've worked out a way to include them in our social life without inflicting them too much on our guests, and I've noticed lots of our friends have arrived at similar arrangements. Most of these suggestions work best with children over the age of five, but I don't recall that we managed to entertain much when the boys were tiny anyway.

Entertaining is by definition out of the ordinary. As you make preparations for your guests, make sure your children know what you expect of them. Run through your plan for the party with them. They should know who's coming and whether or not they've met these people before. I usually try to make sure our children get some kind of treat, too. Since I expect special behavior from them,

I want to reward them for it. And I also want them to have pleasant memories of our grown-up parties. If your children will eat before the adults, give them their favorite meal. If they're going to get to stay up late, make sure they know what a privilege that is.

The more often you have friends over, the more accustomed your children will become to the party routine, but in the beginning you'll have to prompt them, in a quiet voice, to follow these rules:

Greet adult guests.

It isn't necessary to have the kids all dressed up sitting on the doorstep as a welcoming party. But when they wander in from the backyard, they should shake hands with each guest. (See "Meeting People," page 69.)

Submit to small talk.

Many grown-ups can't resist trying to start a conversation with a child. Shy preschoolers can get away with clinging to Dad's leg and peering out at people, but there's a general expectation that a child of six or older should answer a few boring questions like "How old are you now? How do you like school? When did you lose that tooth?" Kids' reactions to this kind of talk varies from barely civil monosyllables to a cheerful torrent of information. (We have one of each in our house.) The older children are, the more poise is expected of them, but often grown-ups ask kids such stupid questions that you can't be surprised if the conversation falls flat. I've noticed that our friends who have children of their own tend to shake hands with Willy and Timo and say, "It's nice to see you again," politely releasing the boys to do something more interesting than talk to adults.

Surrender the living room to the adults,

or whatever room will be used for entertaining. In other words, Charlie shouldn't be sitting in front of the TV playing Sonic Spinball while you and your guests try to discuss mortgage rates. Nor should there be blocks all over the floor or Silly Putty stuck behind the sofa cushions. Nor should Courtney start target practice with her Nerf crossbow just as everybody gets settled with a drink. I'm not saying the kids have to vanish. Just that this is grown-up social time and children can join it, but the principal activity is chatting. Not ducking arrows.

Help out as hosts.

A child of four can pass a bowl of olives to the guests. An older child can take drink orders and relay them to a grown-up in the kitchen. I was a shy child and always hated doing this when I was little, but it's an important lesson in hospitality. We offer guests food and drink. Enlist kids in this activity when they're young so that when they get to be self-conscious preteens, they'll take it for granted as just one more odious job Mom makes them do.

Try not to interrupt grown-up conversation.

The children our generation is raising are both seen and heard, and we wouldn't have it otherwise. But you surely didn't invite other adults over in order to listen to your seven-year-old. It's a good idea for parents to provide some absorbing activity for kids, if possible. A video in the bedroom is a tried and true solution.

Say "Good night" to the guests.

Use your own judgment about how formally kids should take their leave. Some parents have their children go around the room shaking hands with the guests, while others are happy with a general "good night" called from the doorway. I'd say that if you have fewer than six guests, the individual farewell is both courteous and manageable. And then you excuse yourself from your guests to tuck the little ones into bed—and that should be that.

Stay in bed.

This is the stumbling block for a lot of families. A friend of mine recently dined with a couple who were having their first dinner party since having children. Everything went very well, and the children vanished at the correct point in the evening. But the host confessed that he and his wife hadn't quite thought through the evening completely. "We put the children to sleep in our bed as a special treat, and I have no idea where I'm going to sleep tonight," he said.

And of course the nights when you have people over are the nights when your kids need extra drinks of water or have bad dreams or simply can't get to sleep. If you ever have any trouble getting your children to bed (and who doesn't?), it will be magnified by the strange voices in the house and your child's uncanny perception that you will do almost anything to get him to be quiet on this particular night. Timo, at four, used to find imaginary snails and bugs in his bed whenever we had guests. They had to be removed with a whisk broom and a flashlight and of course we scurried around doing his bidding, just to shut him up. Decide ahead how far you are willing to go (Let your child sleep in your bed? Let her stay up till the guests leave? Let her fall asleep in front of the TV?) to buy a little peace and quiet.

Children who participate in their parents' hospitality aren't just making a good impression on your guests. I think they're more likely to be good hosts themselves later in life.

• CRITICAL THINKING •

A friend of mine recently entertained a family of four at his summer cottage. He went outside after dinner to smoke a small, mild-smelling cigar, as is his habit. The ten-year-old girl, his guest, stayed inside, but he was aware of her holding her nose, fanning the air, and making faces of disgust. My friend, her host, found this behavior intolerably rude.

He was right. Sure, smoking is bad for you. And sure, children are by nature puritanical. And yes, they are bombarded with information about a) nutrition and b) the environment, so I think they tend to be a little preoccupied with the weird substances adults like to ingest. ("Is that a beer? Is there alcohol in it? Are you going to get *drunk?*" asks a five-year-old as you pop the top of a nice, cold Bud.)

But let's look for a minute at the nature of criticism. It's never fun to be told that your behavior doesn't measure up. Criticism is easiest to bear when it's gently worded and when it comes from someone you respect. It probably wouldn't be too hard to accept a little advice on your tennis stroke from Chris Evert, for instance.

But children are rarely experts. And their complaints are intended less to help an adult improve than to fix a situation *they* don't like. (Secondhand smoke or a news station on the radio or a burned spot on a hamburger bun.)

You don't want to stifle your children, of course. What you can do is forestall or refocus their complaints. Warn them if you're going to be somewhere with a smoker and point out that for a short while, you all need to tolerate the smoke without mentioning how unhealthy it is. (Many smokers feel pretty defensive these days, so the faintest gesture of disgust from a child will annoy them.) And the next time your son says, "Mom, you're doing it wrong!" stop to discuss how this makes you feel. Embarrassed? Annoyed? How would he feel? Was there another way he could have said that? Is there anything you can do about, say, the burned spot on the hamburger bun? You can cut it off: yes, and so can he. All by himself. Without saying anything about your cooking skills that could hurt your feelings.

If you work now on taming that critical faculty in your children, you might get a few years' reprieve, until the teenagers start in earnest.

Sleepover Manners

The Basic Rules:

Follow the family routine • Eat what's offered • Don't keep the other kids awake • Don't wake anybody up unless there's an emergency • Take home everything you brought • Say "Thank you" when you leave

I remember as a child getting very excited about sleepovers, and my children still think it's a great treat to spend the night at a friend's house or have a pal over here. I'm not quite sure why; it's not as if our normally tame routine erupts with pillow fights and midnight ice cream or even much giggling after lights-out. I suspect the appeal comes from the slight, unthreatening variation from the norm. An extra body breathing slowly in the dark. Cheerios eaten out of a different kind of bowl, the night light in a different place. Somebody to play with at 7 A.M. It's a manageable adventure, and even the adults will find it manageable if your child follows these rules.

Follow the family routine.

Every family does things a little differently. That's part of the appeal of a sleepover. But your child needs to understand that when she's over at Sylvia's house, she goes along with the program. If Sylvia's mother reads a story to the whole family before bed, then a guest should sit and listen. Even if it's a story she knows. Without making too much of an issue out of this, you should mention to your child that when she's a guest, she does what's expected of her. Even if bedtime is earlier than she's used to.

Eat what's offered.

Usually novelty provides enough charm to make meals at someone else's house enticing. A child who wouldn't eat fishsticks at home may find them very glamorous at his friend Patrick's. But even if he doesn't, he should shove them around the plate and eat his vegetables instead. If your child has food allergies, of course you'll discuss that with the host parents before he goes off for the night. Otherwise, he should accept the rations that are doled out.

Don't keep the other kids awake.

A certain amount of giggling and silliness is part of the game plan. But your child should be able to recognize that steely, "Now I'm serious" tone in a grown-up's voice, and cut the cackle. It never hurts to be the first one to buckle under to authority.

Don't wake anybody up unless there's an emergency.

We had a guest over not long ago who woke up at five in the morning and wanted company, so he wakened one of my sons. I felt sorry for him, in a way. It's no joke not being able to sleep. But I wasn't going to have him depriving anybody else of sleep, too. Most children will be a little intimidated by being with another family, so they're unlikely to stir unless they know other folks are awake. Still, it's worth reminding your child how much adults value their sleep. Especially adults who aren't related to them.

Take home everything you brought.

I haven't noticed that eight-year-old boys are particularly good at keeping track of their possessions. (We had one guest who neatly put his dirty clothes in our laundry hamper and I didn't find them until I did the laundry three days later!) But it is annoying for parents to have to return stray toothbrushes and socks to their owners. If you are picking up your child from a sleepover, you can help out by casting a quick glance over his belongings to make sure everything is there.

Say "Thank you" when you leave.

You probably won't be able to guarantee that this happens unless you personally receive your child from the hands of her adult hosts. But you remind your child before you drop her off, and when you see her again, to thank everyone. "Thanks for the sleepover, it was lots of fun!" is fine. I don't think a thank-you note is necessary, but the words must be said.

When your child has these rules down, she's sure to be a welcome guest anywhere, for any (reasonable) length of time.

Getting Around

Hold doors open for grown-ups • Let people get out
before you go in • Wait for your turn • Let someone
who needs help go first • Offer your seat to someone
who needs it • Pay attention to pedestrians • Say
"Excuse me." • Thank people who help you

First we carry our children. Then we hold their hands. Then
we herd them in and out of doors like little ducks, nudging
them in front of us so nobody gets lost. Then, all of a sudden,
they're four feet tall and they're stepping on your toes. Or
careening into old ladies with canes. And you realize that your
children have reached critical mass: They're large enough to do
some damage. It's time to teach them how to navigate in a world
they share with other people.

The biggest challenge is that young children often aren't thoroughly aware of the world around them. They honestly don't see
the man in a hurry who's desperate to get out of the elevator before
they get in. Or the pregnant woman on the bus, sagging with
exhaustion. So your principal job is to pound some sensitivity into
their oblivious little heads. I tend to issue a stream of instructions
as we walk along the street: "Willy, look out for the lady. Timo, let
this gentleman go first. Let the people get *off* the train first, please."
Of course these issues are more pressing in New York, where you
can spot an out-of-towner by the way he walks. So if you can teach
your children these rules, you know they'll pass unobtrusively on
the most congested sidewalk.

Hold doors open for grown-ups.

In Willy's first-grade class, the post of "door holder" was a privilege. He and his brother still argue over who will hold which door to our apartment building, so I get to sail through gracefully, thanking them both. You may have to instruct your child about where to put his body so that someone else can get past, and to extend this courtesy to the next person coming in as well.

Let people get out before you go in.

Or, as they say in that rough-and-ready way on the New York subways, "Let 'em off first." If you don't restrain your children, they will try to push their way into an elevator or onto a bus before anybody has a chance to exit. After a lot of reminders and a frequent hand on his shoulder, Willy finally understands this principle.

Wait for your turn.

Every kindergartner understands waiting in line, but may not realize that you have to do it at movie theaters or in supermarkets as well as in the school lunchroom. Occasional reminders will help your child transfer this skill to life beyond school.

Let someone who needs help go first.

If you make a practice of helping the elderly or the encumbered, you set a great example. Whisper your rationale to your child first: "We'll let this lady go first because her baby is crying and she needs to go home."

Offer your seat to someone who needs it.

Same principle as above. I'm not guaranteeing that when your child is a teenager traveling with his pals he'll remember this, but he *certainly* won't if you never make the gesture yourself.

Pay attention to pedestrians.

This rule is important for children on foot, and even more important for those who travel by skateboard, bicycle, or inline skates. Yet I sometimes despair of ever drumming it into my sons' heads. Will, who wants to be a football player, threads his way through the cracks in the sidewalk to improve his footwork. Timo may walk normally, or he may dance or creep along like a cheetah. I have a paranoid vision of the two of them racing along the sidewalk cutting down old ladies like bowling balls toppling the pins. So I yell a lot: "Look out for the wheelchair. Pay attention!" I'm hoping the effect is cumulative.

Say "Excuse me" if you bump into someone.

Actually, the children *don't* bump into people very often. Maybe the pedestrians in our neighborhood are more alert than I give them credit for. If your child does jostle someone, or step on their foot, or cause them to drop that paper sack full of ripe tomatoes, she needs to apologize and help repair the damage. Again, you prompt this behavior when your child is with you, just hoping that when you're not around, she'll remember anyway.

Thank people who help you.

Elevator operators, crossing guards, bus drivers, cashiers are not made of stone. They appreciate acknowledgment of their services, and deserve to get it. Ideally, your child will say "Thank you" every time he gets off the school bus. I think the only way to achieve this may be a quick, intensive campaign. Every time you greet your child as he leaves the bus, ask, "Did you say 'Thank you' to the driver?" And you keep it up until the answer is a bored "Yes" for five days in a row. Then you can stop, with occasional refresher inquiries.

A child who follows these rules can negotiate a crowded city sidewalk or the school playground at recess with confidence. The parent of such a child can even be sure that the child on her own is not only *not* causing traffic jams, but may even be amazing teachers and other adults by holding doors open for admiring kindergarteners, a turn of events that makes everyone happy. Including your proudly polite child.

• D O N ' T   G E T   N O   R E S P E C T •

Sooner or later, your child is going to ask, in a fed-up tone of voice, "Why do I have to learn manners anyway?" You may want to end the conversation fast by saying, "People will like you better if you're polite." Or, if it's a quiet moment and you're feeling energetic and Laura seems receptive, you may want to have a little talk about respect.

One of the most important things about good manners is that they express respect for other people. Defining the term isn't easy: Most dictionaries toss around synonyms like "esteem" and "honor," which are useless when you're talking to a child. I think a good way to explain respect to a child is: "Showing that you think somebody else is as important as you are." That doesn't cover the entire sense of the word, but it does emphasize the notion of consideration. Thinking about other people as well as yourself. "How would you feel if . . . ?"

Kids understand this. Lower grade classrooms sometimes display prominent lists of "Class Rules" that the children themselves have written. The rules usually express how the children want to work together in the classroom, and they often include precepts like "No interrupting" and "Don't peek in somebody else's desk." In other words, children should treat each other the way they want to be treated. And it's easy to point out the connection between how children want to be treated in the classroom and how everybody else wants to be treated all the time. We all want to feel that we matter and that our efforts are appreciated. That's why, when you're on your knees in front of your five-year-old child, head bowed in a posture of complete submission, you want her to say, "Thanks for tying my shoes, Daddy."

Computer Courtesy

No food or drink near the computer • No sticky fingers on the keys • Put things back the way they were • No snooping

Generally I think of manners as the way we behave with other people, and most of the guidelines in this book cover direct encounters with human beings. But computers provide contact with people in new, indirect ways. So we need to teach our children how to use computers politely.

I asked the advice of Bruce Stark, president of The Computer Tutor in New York City, since his business as a trainer and consultant on computer use takes him into dozens of homes. "The placement of the computer," Stark points out, "is really important. If the computer is in one child's room, it becomes his and he becomes proprietary about it. But if it's in a central room, a den or a family room, it's understood from the moment it's installed that it's a family item and that nobody can be proprietary about it."

Stark also points out the importance of establishing rules for using the computer, just as you would for the TV. If an older sibling or a parent needs to use the computer for homework or work, that naturally takes precedence over yet another bout with the Flight Simulator. (Parents have to be disciplined about this, too, and yield to a child whose report is due instead of surfing the Net for hours.) If your family enjoys this level of organization, you could work out a sign-up sheet or a system of tokens for computer time that could be traded around.

And then there are ground rules that should be second nature to your children. That means, of course, perpetual reminders. You might even want to post a set of rules near the computer to alert newcomers to your requirements. (Rules for more advanced users are on page 178.) The basics are:

No food or drink near the computer.

You don't even want to know what a can of soda can do to your investment in circuitry. Even crumbs from potato chips have a cumulative effect on moving parts, like keys. Of course this does mean that you can't position your coffee mug right next to the mouse, either. But you probably shouldn't anyway.

No sticky fingers on the keys.

This is the kind of rule that wouldn't occur to someone who has never sat down at a keyboard that had been previously anointed with peanut butter. Keeping computers clean isn't just a matter of aesthetics, it's a matter of survival. You can insist that your children wash—and dry—their hands before they boot up. They won't like it, but stand firm.

Put things back the way they were.

You can't realistically expect a seven-year-old to take her "Reader Rabbit" CD out of the drive and file it. What you can do is *ask* her to do these things, or do them yourself while explaining how important it is to leave a space neat and tidy. Then if she even makes an effort in that direction, like pushing in the chair, praise her. And keep at it.

No snooping.

Computer files are the same as personal papers, and you wouldn't want your child opening the files on your desk and reading them. You just need to make this principle clear to your children. School-age children understand the need for privacy, and most of the time they'll respect it, but for those rare moments when a sense of mischief (or annoyance with the adults) overcomes courtesy, you can make snooping harder. Programs like KidDesk limit children's access to certain files. That's the first line of defense, but most eight-year-olds can figure out how to disable these programs. So the next step is to put a password on private files. As Bruce Stark says, "Any parent who puts a journal on a computer and doesn't password it is crazy." After all, you wouldn't leave your diary lying around open, would you?

Computers will loom larger and larger in our children's lives and it's likely that a whole new system of computer manners will gradually emerge, just as the rules of the road did a hundred years ago. For the time being, though, these elementary steps will be sufficient.

Yucky Food

Intermediate Rules:

Don't say "Yuck," don't make faces • Take three bites • Disguise the fact that you aren't eating

A few years ago my husband and I had dinner with some friends and their Chinese houseguest. It was the day of the Chinese New Year, so Wong Fen had made a special trip to Chinatown to purchase moon cakes, a Chinese delicacy traditionally eaten to celebrate the New Year. I had brought meringues for dessert.

The moon cakes were served at the end of the meal. They were, to our Western palates, weird. (Wong Fen didn't care much for the meringues either.) The texture was very solid yet grainy, and each cake appeared to have an egg yolk at the center. We all said "Oh, how interesting!" and crumbled bits of them, but I noticed that our hostess not only consumed a large piece, but actually took seconds. It was only when Wong Fen was called away to the phone that she revealed her napkin, bulging with moon cake crumbs. We greatly admired her finesse and courtesy to her guest.

Every family needs a yucky-food policy. What's more, it's a little like having a fire evacuation policy at school: You work out the routine and practice it, because you never know when somebody is going to put a plateful of little tiny octopus tentacles in front of your child. Or, more likely, when your child is going to decide that perfectly normal macaroni and cheese is disgusting. Or when there is one lonely poppy seed clinging to an otherwise pristine bagel, making it unfit for juvenile consumption.

The broad outlines are up to you because every family has different food rules. I have to confess that I am an abject pushover about food. (No doubt this is because I was forced to eat cold boiled zucchini as a child.) I can't tolerate strife over eating, so my children get away with being pretty quixotic about what they'll accept. There are, of course, many psychologists who back up this approach; it's the old "let them eat what they want and they'll select the right nutrition" school of thought. All very well, but the psychologists don't say what you're supposed to do when your children sneer at your mother-in-law's meatloaf. I would aim for the following approach:

Don't say "Yuck," don't make faces.

This step requires superhuman self-control. Also practice. Play pretend at home: Tell your child that the bowl of Cheerios you've just given him is actually frog's legs. Discuss all the strange things people eat all over the world. With a precocious child, you might even be able to introduce the concept of subtle irony. I'm not kidding: It might give your child a sense of control over the situation if she can look at a serving of a food that horrifies her and say, lightly, but completely ironically, "Oh, good, liver!"

Take three bites.

This is where I fail completely. And if you know your children won't taste "yucky" food without creating a scene, I would skip this step. The ultimate goal is this scenario is to get down from the dinner table without having upset *anybody*, cook or child. If your family policy requires tasting, though, then you should stick with it.

Disguise the fact that you aren't eating.

There's a fine line between cutting up a brussels sprout to make it look as if you ate some, and playing with your food. Still, I think this is a concept worth introducing. I know a five-year-old who is a selective eater but who, in company, will push things around his plate to make it look as if he's enjoying the meal. No diplomat could do better.

I would not, however, introduce the napkin trick until quite a bit later. Most children will probably discover it on their own, and use it to palm those last few bites of green beans that you were foolish enough to put on their plates.

Playing Games

The Basic Rules:

Don't touch your cards until the dealer finishes • Don't peek at someone else's hand • Hold your cards close to your chest • Hand the dice to the next player • Take the outcome calmly

We have reached the Age of Games in our house. This is a distinct stage, a welcome step beyond being required to play Candy Land until your brain starts to drip out your ears. You'll know you've reached it when your child tries to teach you how to play seven-card stud with twos, nines, and one-eyed jacks all wild. I'm certainly delighted to find common ground with the children. And now that we've logged so many hours over a deck of cards or a pair of dice, I'm acutely aware of certain niceties of play. Not sportsmanship (a separate issue, handled on page 115). Just the little courtesies that make the game run smoother.

Don't touch your cards until the dealer finishes.

Little hands grabbing as the cards fall make most dealers nervous. If you correct your children often enough on this, they'll get the idea. You could even point out that in Las Vegas, where the big gamblers go, dealers won't deal if you touch the cards before they're finished. (I have no idea if this is true, but it sounds good.)

Don't peek at someone else's hand.

This is a matter of honor, and very hard to enforce, especially if you play with preschoolers who have trouble holding more than two or three cards. Just point out that in real games, peeking is considered cheating.

Hold your cards close to your chest.

Make it easy for other people not to see your hand. That's courtesy too, in a complicated grown-up way. Reminders will be necessary until this becomes habit.

Hand the dice to the next player.

You roll, you move your guy, and you gather the dice together and slide them to the person who goes next. This is the kind of classic, thoughtful behavior that can be habit if you remind your child and are scrupulous about practicing it yourself. And believe me, people will give your child a lot of credit for just such small courtesies later in life.

Take the outcome calmly.

No fussing over a loss, no preening over a win. Your example is worth a lot here, and if you can say, "Shucks! You did a great job finding all those kings," your child sees that losing is not a devastating experience. We try to say "Nice game" and shake hands after every game, no matter who wins.

Once this kind of courteous behavior becomes routine for your child, you can go back to concentrating on winning the game!

What Grown-Ups Like

Speak when you're spoken to • Do as you're asked
• Ask nicely • "Please" and "Thank you" are essential • Don't grab

Children don't really care about each other's manners. As long as their interchanges with their friends are fair and basically kind, the niceties don't interest them. So in a way, you are teaching your child good manners for the benefit of the grown-ups she encounters (both when she's a child and when she's a grown-up herself). Maybe this seems a little ludicrous. After all, adults should like children and make allowances for them. But the fact is, they often don't. And another fact is that as your child gets older and older, grown-ups other than yourself will not only have more contact with your child, but also can materially affect her fate. If your daughter's second-grade teacher thinks she's sassy, it's going to be a miserable school year. And if your son's best friend's mother thinks your son is obnoxious, they'll be doing most of their playing at your house.

And you know what? There is nothing wrong with adults requiring a little respect from children. We have lived longer than they have, we are wiser. We possess the bank cards and the car keys. It is perfectly legitimate for adults to expect certain courtesies from children. Here are some behaviors that you should routinely insist on from your children, so that they'll routinely behave this way with other adults. The big exception, of course, especially to the first two points, is when your child interacts with strangers. (See page 185 for some pointers on combining courtesy with safety.)

Speak when you're spoken to.

It's understandable for a preschooler to be paralyzed with shyness, but a child of six or more must answer an adult's greeting or question. Point out to your child how hurtful it is when her friends ignore her. You could even role-play, just to get across the point that not responding makes the questioner feel really stupid and uncomfortable, and nobody likes that.

This can be hard for shy children, but even a muttered monosyllabic response is better than nothing. If a child is clearly uncomfortable talking to an adult it's pretty obvious, and most grown-ups are sensitive enough to let a shy child off the hook and stop torturing her with questions.

Do as you're asked.

This seems like a pretty obvious point, but compliance isn't always a sure thing. Last week, as I was bringing my children inside from the park, I asked an eight-year-old pal of Willy's to give me our football. In response, he threw it in the air. Fortunately for my dignity I managed to catch it, but I was not charmed.

Ask nicely.

Kids need grown-ups to do lots of things for them: get the backpack out of the trunk, turn the sweater right side out, unravel a fiendish knot in a shoelace. Nobody minds this, it's part of the job. But it helps a lot if the request is politely phrased. In other words, "May I have some juice, please?" instead of "I want some juice." Or "Can we play on the computer?" instead of "We want to play on the computer." Real sticklers prefer "May" to "Can."

You may have to stop your child each time you get the boorish "I wanna" and say, "Can you please think of another way to ask that?" A diffident or precocious child may catch onto "Could you. . . ." "Would you mind. . . ." "Do you think you could. . . ." if you use these phrases, but they aren't necessary.

"Please" and "Thank you" are essential.

Enough said.

Don't grab.

Sometimes when I get a box of cookies down from the cupboard I feel as if I'm holding a plate of dog biscuits just out of reach of a howling pack of puppies. These little hands come from nowhere, and before I know it the box is on the floor. My ideal is to have the children sitting at the table, waiting for me to put a plate of cookies in front of them. We're still working on this, and it's simply a matter of constant reminding—then witholding the reward until the desired behavior is achieved. They sit, they get cookies. If a dog can figure this out, so can a child.

We've come a long way from the days when children were supposed to be seen but not heard—possibly too far. It's time to backtrack a bit and insist on a little bit of deference for the grown-ups. Yes, that means us!

• RISE AND SHINE •

When I was a child, we stood up every time an adult entered the classroom, as a mark of respect to that grown-up. In fact, throughout life, you're supposed to stand up to indicate respect for a social superior. Some of that etiquette lingers in formal offices, where you'd never dream of sitting down in the boss's office before she asked you to. We lead a pretty informal life, so I have not taught my sons to rise when an adult enters the room. But Marguerite Kelly (who wrote *The Family Almanac* among other useful books) thinks children should get up for adults. And I am reconsidering my point of view. Just a few days ago our neighbor dropped in to say hello. Timothy, who is extremely social and outgoing, hopped out of his chair and rushed to give her a hug. Willy, completely engrossed in the sports pages, didn't even look up as he muttered, "Hi." I know which greeting I'd prefer. If you decide that this attractive habit would suit your family, here's Kelly's method for teaching it. She suggests that adults help kids rise to the occasion (sorry) by walking over to them and sticking out a hand, just out of reach, so the child has to stand up to shake hands. Then the grown-up can be very impressed by the child's courtesy, and the child will be, too. Unfortunately, not all the adults you see will have had this training, so you might have to introduce the idea. The most positive way to do this would be to say, "It's so nice when children stand up to say hello to a grown-up. Let's remember to try that." You can practice, if your child doesn't think role-playing is ridiculous. And the next time your doorbell rings, remind your child that you want her to put down Barbie for a second or pause her video game, stand up and shake hands or say hello, and then go back to what she was doing. Having made a wonderful impression on your visitors.

Talking about Money

Don't ask what other people's things cost • Don't offer information about how much things that *you* own cost • Don't share family financial information with your friends • Never tease anyone about their financial situation

I was brought up with the notion that talking about money was rude. You never mentioned what things cost or how much money people had, or made. (Little did I know that grown-ups discussed money all the time, just in a veiled way.)

I still get a little shock when people put prices on things in conversation. On the other hand, I think a complete ban on financial talk is unrealistic. We don't want our children to feel that money is a taboo topic. Kids must understand how money works. But you don't want them going through life like little appraisers, mentally costing everything from their new barrettes to their best friend's parents' car.

Mind you, many children go through a phase, or several phases, when they come to grips with money and what it can do. When you start giving your child an allowance, she may want to know what every single one of her toys cost. She's trying to assess the buying power of that allowance. An older child will broaden his frame of reference and start looking at the price tags on sneakers, for instance. Part of what he's doing is calculating what his pal's Air Jordans are worth. And that's appropriate. Grown-ups do this all the time. Why else would we wear clothes with somebody else's initials on them? A logo is just a price tag, in code. The trick is that, hypocritical or not, our culture requires that the price tags on things stay in code.

It's hard to come up with sensible, consistent rules about this issue because society's rules are so subtle. You can talk about how much your neighbors sold *their* house for, but you can't talk about what you paid for your own. The rules also vary from one subculture to the next. I've lived in New York long enough to lose some of my WASP reticence about money matters. I've caught myself bragging about how little I paid for a Calvin Klein jacket at a discount store. Yet I've seen my southern friends flinch when I mention the price of something mundane like milk. So you may want to refine these guidelines according to your own circumstances. In any case, they should prevent your children from appearing to be completely mercenary.

Don't ask what other people's things cost.

Let's say Alana turns up on the first day of kindergarten in a new velour dress. Kimberley falls in love with this dress. She can say she likes it and she can ask where Alana got it. She cannot ask, "How much was it?"

Now, here comes the complicated part. Kimberley's mother, being a sophisticated adult, could go a step further and ask what brand it is, which, if she's a clever consumer, will give her ball-park information on price. She could even, in some circles, say, "Oh, that Guess stuff is so cute but it's awfully expensive." This is a broad hint, and Alana's mom can take it or not. If she doesn't, Kimberley's mom has no further recourse. She has to call a retailer to get the numbers.

I'm going into this kind of detail only to demonstrate that delicate angling for financial information is beyond the reach of most children. And anything more obvious is not generally considered polite. The one exception is that you can ask what things cost in a *general* way. For instance, Todd can say to Sam, "I want to save my birthday money to buy Game Boy. Do you know how much it costs?" Todd is not saying directly, "How much did you pay for Game Boy?"

because that would be rude. The bottom-line taboo is putting a price on things people possess, whether it's their clothes or their furniture or their pure-bred Great Dane.

Don't offer information about how much things that *you* own cost.

This is bragging. (Equally bad is my besetting sin, bragging about how *little* things cost, but kids don't generally do that.) What you want to avoid is Joseph proudly showing his new bike to Paul and saying, "It cost a hundred dollars!" The reasoning is that maybe Paul or his parents couldn't afford a hundred-dollar bike and this will make them feel uncomfortable.

Don't share family financial information with your friends.

I don't think it makes much sense for children under twelve to know the details of their family's finances because they can't put these numbers into perspective. But if you do include a child in discussions of how to spend your vacation budget, for instance, you should also stress that these are private conversations and shouldn't go outside the family.

Never tease anyone about their financial situation.

Whether people have less money than you or more, it's rarely something they can laugh about.

Children in elementary school are instinctively aware of money's emotional power, so teaching them discretion about it is fairly straightforward. You can simply tell them what the rules are, and issue a reminder or two as needed. Appealing to empathy and warnings about showing off should clinch the deal.

PART III

Young Sophisticates

Ages 10-12

Ten is big. Ten-year-olds get around on their own and have lots of homework and busy schedules. They think they know everything, and they certainly know lots of things that their parents don't know, like the names of the cool bands, the latest ruinous statistics about the environment, and how to hook up the computer to answer your phone. But every now and then they get caught up short, and realize that they don't know *every-thing*—yet. That's when they still need their parents.

By the time they reach fifth grade, most kids have had some serious indoctrination into good manners. With luck, lots of the coaching has taken root, because ill-mannered preteens seem especially boorish. What's more, grown-ups they don't even know very well feel entitled to correct their manners. A neighborhood boy was here the other day, and when he called his mother's office, he said, "Hi, this is Larry. Can I speak to Suzette?" There was a short pause. "Please," he added, clearly at the prompting of the receptionist. And he seemed embarrassed. Most children would rather have corrections like that coming from their parents than from people who barely know them.

If you haven't put a lot of effort into teaching the rules presented in Parts I and II, now is the time to start. Your children spend more time than ever interacting with adults they aren't related to, and good manners count a lot toward making those interactions more pleasant. Your child may have the best heart in the world, but the people she deals with won't be able to see past what they consider uncouth behavior. Saying please and thank you, basic table manners, considerate use of physical space, and telephone courtesy are essential to comfortable contact with nonfamily adults. Even peers are more observant, and more critical of rough-edged behavior.

At the same time, preteens are interested in acquiring a bit more savoir faire. Most of the rules in this part of the book concern refinements to manners that kids should already have learned. They're either aimed at smoothing out relationships with the outside world, keeping things pleasant within the family, or establishing habits that will be handy in later life. (A few sections deal with entirely new situations that won't arise with younger kids.) In theory, basic good manners are already in place so you no longer have to remind and remind. You're more of a coach now, giving advice and offering strategy, as well as countering resistance to the discipline of learning manners.

Most coaches don't claim authority over their players' entire lives. As Manners Coach, you can't either. A split between peer-group behavior and behavior with adults may appear as your child hits the preteen years. Don't worry too much about the slouching and slang and giggling. It's the adult-world behavior that concerns you, since that's what you're preparing your child for in the long run.

Meeting People

Advanced Rules:

Tell your friends each other's names • Explain how you know each friend • Introduce yourself if nobody else does

In Part II, I discussed how kids should introduce friends and parents. The ultimate goal is actually for them to introduce their friends to each other. It doesn't sound that complicated, does it? All Alice has to do is say, "Terri, this is Isabel." But there are a couple of refinements. And the big hurdle is remembering to do it.

Tell your friends each other's names.

If you have successfully drilled your child in the importance of introducing her friends to you, she will already be sensitive to the premise that people like to be identified, not ignored. What's more, many kids enjoy mixing their friends from different contexts, so that their school pals meet their street hockey buddies. When this kind of mingling is imminent, draw your child aside and say, "You need to be sure to introduce Regina to Polly. Do you know how to do that? Just say, 'Regina, this is Polly. Polly, this is Regina.'" Manners books for adults are still full of formal details: the social inferior is supposed to be presented to the social superior, but it's a little hard to discern social ranking among eleven-year-olds with ponytails, so I don't believe it matters whose name gets said first.

Some children will be able to manage the introductions easily: I know precocious eight-year-olds who already sound like Johnny

Carson as they make all their acquaintances known to each other. Other kids will find the habit difficult to acquire, but I promise, practice does smooth out the awkwardness. What's more, taking the plunge and introducing people avoids the awkwardness of people hanging around eyeing each other, wondering who everybody is.

Explain how you know each friend.

A little additional information can be helpful, too. Really adroit hostesses always add a bit of background to their introductions to help strangers start a conversation. "Mr. Lawrence just came back from New Delhi. . . . Miss Adair is a great rock climber." Children can do this too, in a simpler fashion. "David lives next door," or "Andreina is in my class at school." Kids usually accept each other at face value, without much curiosity about anything beyond the current situation: This is Ali, he has a football, let's play. But putting their friends into context for each other is an extremely courteous habit that will win them a great deal of appreciation as adults.

Introduce yourself if nobody else does.

It took me about thirty-five years to be able to put out my hand to a stranger and say, "I don't think we've met, I'm Carol Wallace." And my social skills are pretty good. Some people, of any age, are simply too shy or reserved to be able to put themselves forward with an introduction. But you can certainly tell your poised and outgoing child that she doesn't have to wait to be introduced to someone. She can take matters into her own capable hands.

The final step in learning about polite meetings and introductions is the biggest hurdle of all: introducing two people whose names you've forgotten. High as my standards are, I'd excuse any child from handling this awkward situation. Anyway, children aren't likely to encounter it because they have one great advantage over adults when it comes to manners. Their memories are much better than ours.

Table Manners

Take your cues from the hostess • Use cutlery from the outside in • Spoon soup away from you • Offer serving plates to your neighbors first • Salt and pepper are passed together • Bread is meant to be broken • Don't crumple your napkin or blow your nose on it • Don't drink from the finger bowls

By the time a child is ten, eating a meal with him should not be a horrifying process. Clumsiness goes with the prepubescent territory, but even the gangliest, most awkward eleven-year old should no longer be uncouth. He should sit straight at the table, putting his napkin in his lap. He should use his utensils correctly, chew with his mouth closed, take moderately sized bites, and talk only when there's no food in his mouth. The napkin should be used frequently. Drinks should be sipped, not quaffed. And when your darling has exhibited enormous restraint and skill throughout the meal and is finally finished, he should ask to be excused and clear his place.

It's a lot to ask. On the other hand, so is long division, and I've certainly found table manners more useful in daily life. What's more, as you round the bend of the latency years and see adolescence sneaking into sight, the issue of table manners becomes more urgent, for two reasons. First, of course, is the notoriously rebellious attitude of teenagers. Your child will do everything in her power to distance herself from you. In her quest toward this goal my older sister became a radical vegetarian and ate only blackish messes from a special hand-thrown bowl, with her own lacquer chopsticks (and that was while she still deigned to live at home). If you missed any of the finer points of table manners while your child was still relatively tractable, you can forget about introducing them during the Years of the Raging Hormones.

The second reason for urgency is more positive. Preadolescence is a time of enormous self-consciousness. What your child wants, above everything else, is to be accepted as one of the group. You can't ensure that, of course; neither can I. And I do realize that very formal manners will brand your child as a geek (or dork or nerd) and doom her to outsider status. However, confidence and *savoir faire* are also urgently needed at this age. It's unlikely that your preteen is ever going to have to eat a quail correctly. But on the other hand, if she goes over to dinner at her boyfriend's house, the ordeal will be a lot easier if she doesn't have to worry about her table manners. For the unsure and self-conscious, eating and drinking are mine fields of potential embarrassment. You wouldn't let your child grow up unable to ride a bike. So do her the favor of giving her eating skills, too.

Most of the suggestions here are refinements. Frankly, if your son or daughter is perfectly comfortable with the guidelines in Parts I and II, she'll manage just fine. She may feel out of her depth in a formal situation, though. So why not go the step further and equip her for those occasions?

To give your children practice in a formal way of eating, you have to produce a somewhat more formal atmosphere at home from time to time. You can do this without much trouble. Start by using candles. It's amazing how festive and civilized everything looks once the lights are dimmed. Set the table with an extra fork, and serve salad on separate plates, after the main course. (Yes, this does mean more dishes to wash.) Wrap a few rolls in a napkin on a plate and put a butter dish on the table. If there's room and you don't mind washing them, you could even use bread and butter plates. The whole idea is to get your child used to a more complex, cluttered place setting. It doesn't even have to be the same each time. There are many variations on the basic theme of formal dining, and if you teach your child to cope comfortably with them, that's all to the good.

Of course this is not how your child eats among her friends. By the time kids reach their preteens, there is a great gulf between their behavior for adults (including language and clothes and table manners) and their behavior among themselves. Does your daughter even use a fork or spoon when she's eating lunch at school? Don't bet on it. But rest assured that she *can* switch comfortably between kid behavior and behavior for the grown-ups. She hasn't forgotten all the manners you ever taught her. And she's ready to learn some more advanced skills, like the following:

Take your cues from the hostess.

This means the female grown-up in charge, whether it's Dad's girlfriend or the First Lady. Nobody eats until she picks up her fork. If the guests are wondering how to handle that shellfish in the soup, they check to see how she does it. They copy how she handles her bread and her salad fork. Following her lead, it's impossible to go wrong.

Use cutlery from the outside in.

In other words, when you sit down to a confusing array of forks and spoons and knives, you use the first ones that come to hand. The fork farthest from the left-hand side of the plate, the farthest spoon from the right. You can reinforce this rule when you show your child how to set the table for a formal dinner. You don't have to have fancy silver and it most certainly doesn't matter if all the knives and forks match. But a salad fork is smaller than a dinner fork because it doesn't have to do the same kind of heavy lifting. And a soup spoon is bigger than a teaspoon because if you ate soup with a teaspoon you'd be sitting at the table all night. Form follows function.

So if your child sits down and notices that her place setting has a big fork next to the napkin and a little fork next to the plate, she knows she's going to use the big fork first. If there are a spoon and fork lying above the plate, they are for dessert.

Spoon soup away from you.

Kids should know that there's a practical reason for this. You fill your spoon by dragging it across the bowl *away* from you so that you don't create a small tidal wave of tomato bisque that will splash into your lap. For the same reason, you can lightly scrape the bowl of your spoon across the far edge of your bowl. This action will catch the drips. If more grown men had acquired this habit as children their ties would last a lot longer.

Offer serving plates to your neighbors first.

In other words, if the salad bowl starts at your child's end of the table, he offers it to his neighbor before helping himself. Of course, it's always possible that his neighbor, not being as well brought up as he is, will then pass the bowl away from him and he won't get any salad. He can always ask to have it sent back. (Please.)

Salt and pepper are passed together.

This is an old superstition. If somebody asks you for one, you pass both. And you are careful to put them down on the table for your neighbor to pick up, instead of placing them directly into your neighbor's hand, which would be bad luck. Look, it can't hurt. Though frankly I wouldn't spend too much breath nagging my children about this one.

Bread is meant to be broken.

The polite way to handle bread or rolls is to break them into small pieces and butter each piece before it's eaten. Diners should put a pat of butter onto their plates so they don't keep dipping into the communal butter dish. One blunt way to remind your child about this is to point out that nobody's making sandwiches here: You don't butter the whole slice of bread as if you were about to put on the salami. Another reminder that may work: If you butter only a little piece at a time, there's less of a chance that it'll fall on the floor, butter side down.

Don't crumple your napkin or blow your nose on it.

A napkin that has been spread on a lap and used to dab gently at a mouth will show signs of wear, sure, but not signs of stress. And it would be a pity to get through a formal meal with elegance and spoil the picture by what you leave behind. If you catch your child in napkin abuse, point it out.

Don't drink from the finger bowls.

A finger bowl is a shallow bowl full of warm water that is placed in front of diners after the salad course and before dessert. There's an apocryphal story about an ignorant guest at the White House who lifted the bowl to his mouth and drank the contents (and the hostess followed suit, to make him feel at ease). You don't have to believe it to tell it to your children.

The correct way to handle a finger bowl, of course, is to dabble your fingertips in the warm water and dry them on your napkin. Then you carefully remove the bowl (and doily if there was one) from the plate it came in on, and set it on the table in front of you. The waiter (you have to have a waiter to bother with finger bowls) will come and take it away. The plate is now your dessert plate.

This custom predates forks and spoons and you can imagine that in the bad old days of eating with one's fingers, a finger bowl came in handy. Now they are rarely seen and unless you meet up with them at the dinner table of a very rich and old-fashioned octogenarian, I'd have to say they're pretty pretentious. Still, you may want to go through the drill once or twice to make your children familiar with it. All you have to do is float a slice of lemon or a geranium leaf on top of some warm water in a soup bowl and stick it on a dessert plate. (True finger bowls are quite shallow, but only great-grandmothers and four-star restaurants own them.)

I suspect finger bowls are going to be pretty scarce in the twenty-first century, so your son or daughter may never need to know how to use one. Still, they say in America any child could become President. If you teach your kids the manners suggested here, a State Dinner at the White House will never intimidate them.

• FANCY FOODS •

One of the few scenes I remember from the TV series "The Little Rascals" is an episode where Alfalfa encounters an artichoke for the first time. He nudges it gently with his fork. It rolls off the plate. He tries to spear it. It resists. This goes on and on for some time and it never occurs to the poor child to attack it the way Emily Post would: with his fingers.

Of course you've told your child that if she's in any doubt about how to eat something she should watch her hostess. But in case you want to practice at home, here are a few techniques for tricky foods.

Artichokes:

Pull the leaves off with your fingers. Dip in sauce, if there is any. Nibble the end of the leaf. Discard it on the edge of your plate. When you get down to the hairy center, scrape it off the heart with the side of your fork. Then you finally use your fork and knife to cut and dip the heart into the sauce.

Oysters:

Pick up with one hand. Loosen the mollusk from the shell by scraping beneath it with a fork. Then lift it to your mouth and slurp. The noise is unavoidable.

Spare ribs:

Pick them up with your fingers. It's the only way you'll get even a shred of meat off them.

Soft-shell crabs:

Eat the whole thing. The shell tastes a little bit like tortilla chips.

Shrimp with shells on:

With your fingers pull off the legs first, then peel off the shell. Hold by the tail to eat, and discard the tail with the shells. Not neat food.

Other shellfish in the shell:

Steady the shell with one hand while you scrape out the creature and eat it with your fork. If they're in soup, this is just too messy to perform politely, so ignore them.

Bony fish:

Remove as many bones as possible with fork and knife. If you come across little bones in your mouth, work them toward the front and push them out discreetly with your tongue. Take them out with your fork and put them on the side of your plate.

Chicken with bones and lamb chops:

Cut off as much meat as you can. Watch your hostess carefully. If she's feeling casual she may pick up her bone to gnaw it, and then you can, too. But if she leaves those last delectable morsels clinging to the bone, you have to as well.

Lemon sections (to squeeze on fish):

Poke the flesh with a fork to make holes for the juice to come out. Then squeeze, cupping your spare hand over the lemon so that the juice doesn't squirt into your neighbor's eye.

Manners of Speech

Advanced Rules:

Keep it clean • If you can't say anything nice, don't say anything at all • If you must tease, do it carefully • Avoid personal remarks, unless they're compliments • Keep your voice down

Remember when kids' mouths got washed out with soap? Has it occurred to you lately that maybe your child needs the same treatment? Not really—it's invasive and unpleasant—but as children pull into the preteen years, there will certainly be times when you can't believe what they say.

Before you start to worry too much about your child's mouth, however, remember that at this age kids speak two parallel languages, one for grown-ups and another among their friends. What you hear coming from the backseat as you drive the boys home from a hockey game may appall you. But poor grammar, bizarre slang, and strange intonations (remember Valley Girl talk, in which every sentence sounds like a question?) shouldn't bother you. Neither should the annoying verbal habits that children pick up from popular culture. Above all, please don't try to sound cool by adopting juvenile mannerisms. Your task as a parent is to maintain the high ground of Standard Spoken English.

This language, as spoken by your children, should include a liberal sprinkling of automatic "pleases" and "thank yous," as well as familiarity with the meaningless but polite exchanges grown-ups trade every day. "Hi, how are you? Fine, how are you?" They shouldn't interrupt unless you've failed to notice the blue and white flashing lights behind you on the highway, and even then they should say, "Excuse me, Mom? Did you notice the cop behind you?"

And there are a few refinements that people expect in conversation with older children and adults. It's time to introduce the following notions.

Keep it clean.

To a ten-year-old, swearing or foul language may seem swashbuckling and debonair. Which of course it isn't, but I don't think you'll convince a child of that. What's more, you shouldn't even attempt to control what your child says out of your presence. But you can make it plain that around you and other grown-ups, certain words just aren't allowed. One good way to stamp out ugly language is to impose a penalty system. Have your child deposit a quarter in a jar every time you catch him using some of those words you dislike. This might work even better if you enlisted *his* help to erase ugly words from your vocabulary as well, making it a joint effort instead of a situation where you're policing him. It may also be helpful if you come up with some alternative expletives. Even a mild word like "Rats!" delivered with gusto can be very expressive.

If you can't say anything nice, don't say anything at all.

Actually the world would be a much less interesting place if people stuck with this rule, but it's a very sensible operating system for kids dealing with the shifting social patterns of middle school. And, boy, does this policy ever make you popular! There's nothing like a positive outlook for attracting friends. I don't mean by this that children should be forbidden to talk about their struggles; merely that catty complaints aren't constructive.

If you must tease, do it carefully.

Affectionate teasing can be heartwarming because it demonstrates to the "victim" that the teaser really knows her and appreciates her. For instance, Martha says to Maria, "Gee, I'd better get off the phone so you can study for that spelling test tomorrow." If

Maria has never had a grade below 95 in spelling, that's affecionate teasing. The teaser must let the victim know that *she doesn't really mean it.* Tone of voice or facial expression would convey this. If teasing is done in this spirit, even adults find it very charming.

What's not charming is teasing intended to wound. Or even clumsily delivered. And unfortunately, it's hard to know in advance what people are going to be sensitive about. One rule of thumb that you can share with your child: Never tease anybody about something that's a genuine shortcoming, unless you know they aren't sensitive about it. Don't tease a klutz about being clumsy or a plump person about his weight. And when in doubt, don't do it at all.

Avoid personal remarks, unless they're compliments.

"I like the color of your hair" is pleasant. "Is it natural?" is not. Most preteens are too inhibited to dream of making this kind of comment, but they should be warned anyway or they may produce a real whopper some time, like "What happened to your leg?"

Keep your voice down.

Back to the "inside voices" of preschool. I once sat in a meeting with a very polished attorney and noticed how, when he wanted attention, he spoke very quietly and unemphatically. Everybody shut up and strained to listen. This is a trick you can use on your children, and you can teach it to them, too.

As children become more and more independent, they have to rely on their own powers of persuasion and argument to deal with people in a friendly fashion and to get what they want. They're bound to make mistakes from time to time, but these rules will help them manage politely.

• WITH YOUNGER CHILDREN •

If your children are frequently around significantly smaller kids, you can probably skip this section because you will have drilled this behavior into them anyway. But sometimes only children (or children who are themselves the youngest siblings) get very large without much sense of how to treat the very small. For instance:

Be gentle.

An affectionate squeeze is lovely, but only if the squeezed child doesn't feel crushed. Rough and tumble games may need to be moderated for smaller bodies, too.

Don't make fun of immaturity.

Older kids should never mock a smaller child's lack of skill with a jump rope or fondness for a blanket or inability to pronounce the letter "R."

Be patient.

It takes a five-year-old longer to see if he has any sixes in his hand, or to walk a block and a half. Adults may need to remind big kids that they, too, were young once.

Be tolerant.

A smaller child who tags along after an older one may be irritating, but she's also paying the big kid a huge compliment. An adult may need to point this out, and to suggest a way that an older child can help a little one feel included without being actually inconvenient. Will and his friends love to play football and they are very kind about bringing Timo into the game without letting him ruin key plays. ("You wanna play special teams, Timo?") It took some prodding from me, but I think even *they* appreciate how kind and generous they're being.

Play Dates

Advanced Rules:

Ask before using the phone • Ask before eating anything • Hosts should offer food and drink • Ask before turning anything on • Put away anything you take out

By the time children get to be ten or more, you can't always call what they do together "playing." So when they have pals over, they aren't really "play dates." But they depend on each other's company more than ever. You may find that you either have no children at home, or you have twice the usual number, since by this age many kids get around on their own and are free to wander from one kid's home to another until they find out who has the best stuff in the refrigerator.

You may never know where your child has been by the time she saunters in for dinner. You won't know who she was with, what she ate, what she said, or what she did. You have to hope, though, that while she was in someone else's house, she paid attention to the rules that follow.

Since you aren't there to monitor behavior, you'll need to let your child know what the guidelines are. Most of the play-date guidelines in Parts I and II have to do with the logistics of invitations and choosing what to play. Those issues don't matter so much with older children. Instead, you're working on forming your child into a good guest. You would hope that anybody who comes into your house would act the same way: The basic principle is that he should remember he's a guest and not make himself too much at home. This won't be a problem for most kids, who are a bit hesitant off their own turf. But if you have an exuberant, outgoing child, you may need to remind her about these limits from time to time. You can also gently correct a child who goes a little too far in your house. "Benita, I wish you'd ask me before helping yourself to a snack," is a completely legitimate comment. Insist, in your house, on the kind of behavior you want your child to exhibit. Like this:

Ask before using the phone.

Think about it. Even a really close adult friend will say, as she reaches for the receiver to make a quick local call, "May I use the phone?" I think we're particularly scrupulous about phone use because telephone calls used to be so expensive, and because the phone is a lifeline for us. An eleven-year-old guest is unlikely to do anything besides call her mother to say where she is, but she should ask first. If she doesn't, you can always say, "Would you like to use the phone?" as she starts to dial.

Ask before eating anything.

We once had a guest for Thanksgiving who hovered over me as I carved the turkey, grabbing little bits of skin and meat from the cutting board. He finally just seized the drumstick and ate it over the sink as I looked on in shock. I'm always glad when people feel comfortable in our apartment, but this was taking things much too far. I have echoes of that outraged feeling when I even think about a child casually opening my refrigerator and pouring a glass of milk without consulting me first. All they have to do is ask. And say please.

Hosts should offer food and drink.

The lovely old rules of hospitality have broken down considerably, but it's still a kind gesture to say to a guest, "Can I get you a drink? Would you like something to eat?" A guest is only supposed to respond to a specific offer, so a thoughtful host presents a range of options: "We have juice, soda, milk, iced tea. . . ." It is especially rude to eat or drink something without offering any of it to your guest.

Ask before turning anything on.

A guest is supposed to be grateful for hospitality. A guest is not supposed to amend the hospitality he's receiving. Which is why he can't turn on the fan or the stereo when he's in someone else's house. Even if it's the bottom of the eighth in the World Series and the score is tied, a guest needs to say, "Would you mind terribly if I just turned the radio on to catch the score?" The TV, because it's so hypnotic, is even further off limits.

Put away anything you take out.

By the age of ten, your children should already be trained to put away the Monopoly pieces or the CDs when they're finished with them. Cleanup after a game at home is a good opportunity for you to say to your child, "I sure hope you clean up after yourself at Philip's house."

These rules, of course, also apply to grown-ups. So once you're sure your child is following them, you'll know he can go anywhere and be a welcome guest.

Telephone Manners

Whose phone is it, anyway, you'll wonder, as for the fourth time in a day you hear yourself saying, "Erica! It's for you!" Communication with peers is the most important thing in life at this age, and this urgency is only going to intensify in the teen years.

Some parents prefer not to fight over maintaining the lines of communication to the outside world and install a children's phone. I'm inclined to think that there are a lot of useful lessons to be learned (cooperation, for example) from working out a way for adults and kids to share one line. If there is a separate children's line, you have no way to monitor phone manners and not much business doing so. But if your children are using your line, there is a definite need for mutual courtesy.

This may be a time in your life, by the way, when Call Waiting becomes a good idea. Many people object to it because they feel it's innately rude. But it could be a lifesaver, especially for working parents trying to reach their children after school. Your child comes home and calls a friend. (You get a busy signal.) They chat for a while (bzzz-bzzz, bzzz-bzzz). They agree to meet at the mall. You call home ten minutes later and the machine picks up. Not helpful.

No matter how simple or elaborate your communications equipment, your children should have mastered the phone manners set out in Parts I and II. When children place calls, they should identify themselves, ask courteously for their friends, politely request that a message be taken. When answering the phone at home, they should ask the caller to wait while they go to get the person who's wanted on the phone, or else offer to take a message. Children should never hang up the phone without saying "Good-bye."

By the age of ten, your child should certainly have all those principles firmly under control. The only refinement I would add is the following radical notion:

Adult calls take precedence.

Wow! The temerity of it: putting grown-ups first! This means that if Mack is on the phone when a call for you comes in, he should let you take your call, and call his friend back later. This may sound a little severe, but imagine the alternative. One of your friends dials your number. Your daughter answers and says, "I'm on the phone right now, can she call you back?" Your daughter has been perfectly polite, but what she has said to your caller is, in effect, "I'm more important than you are." This will not go over big with most people you know.

The grown-ups-first policy isn't going to be popular with your children, but you can always fall back on the age-old rationale: Who, after all, pays the phone bill?

In the Car

Your child will spend a lot of time in other people's cars over the next few years, and it would be nice to know that the people who drive her around think she has good manners. At this age you should be able to take for granted that she'll cooperate on basics like buckling seat belts and not hitting neighbors. What really needs work is civility toward the driver. A pleasant "hello" and a "thank you" at the end of the ride will go a long way with most adults. But kids between ten and twelve can be extremely inconsiderate. It sometimes seems that they think everyone around them had been put on earth only to make their life comfortable.

If your child follows these rules, though, she'll be welcome in any car pool. The trick is, you won't be around to make sure she behaves this way, so you won't have the opportunity to remind her to thank the driver when she gets out of the car. What you can do is insist that the kids *you* drive toe the line. You might even want to have a session at the beginning of the school year (or swimming season or whatever) when you run through your expectations with your passengers. Solicit their suggestions, too:

Sometimes kids demand things of themselves that you wouldn't dream of suggesting.

Do not offer rides to other children without consulting the driver.

"Hi, this is Jenna, she needs to be dropped off by the drugstore." Say *what*? A child may tell her own parent that Jenna has been stranded, and ask if Mom could possibly help out by dropping Jenna off. A really canny child could conspire with the offspring of the driving parent and get *this* kid to ask her Mom to give Jenna a ride. But a car pool is a web of favors owed and given, and kids who ask further favors of drivers not related to them are really pushing their luck.

Do not request changes that lengthen the route.

A child may ask to be let off at a spot that is directly on the route home. A child may not ask to be driven farther than the last stop. If a desperate mother wants to call another mother and ask if, this once, Robin could be taken to her piano lesson, that's between the moms.

Don't expect the car pool to transport pets, sports equipment, or bulky school projects, without warning.

Obviously if this is a football team the drivers are allowing room for the pads. But a parent with a small sedan shouldn't be expected to make room for a diorama of Monticello.

No bathroom talk.

The driver gets to set the standards for language. If she doesn't like hearing the lyrics of gangsta rap songs, she should only have to say so once. Ten- to twelve-year-olds begin to experiment with words much the way they did as preschoolers. They're gauging the power of language to draw a reaction. Don't disappoint them. If you find four-letter words offensive, give those kids the satisfaction of knowing it!

Don't touch the radio dial.

The person who paid for the car (not to mention the gas) gets to choose the music. Period.

Don't criticize the music.

So Gordon Lightfoot is incredibly sappy. (I don't even know the words kids would use to indicate contempt!) So what? You wanna walk home?

Ask permission before eating in the car.

I can imagine a car full of enormous boys eating meatball heroes as I drive them home from soccer. I hope I'll have the strength to tolerate torture like this. It will be easier if the boys say, "Mrs. Hamlin, I missed lunch, do you mind if I eat a sandwich on the way home?"

Don't leave any litter.

Some kids seem to regard cars as mobile garbage cans, but I don't know a single soul whose idea of a good time is cleaning crumpled McDonald's wrappers out of the backseat. A car should be treated like a campsite in the wilderness: You pack out what you pack in.

Don't criticize the car or the way it's driven.

By the age of eleven or twelve, many kids will be conscious of the status values of different models of cars. In an ideal world, all preteen boys would be able to go everywhere in hot red two-seaters. But life forces them to settle for navy blue minivans. This is cruel, I know, but they have to swallow their disappointment stoically. What's more, they must not say a word about the way the van is being driven. (Too slowly, for sure.) Or they risk being dumped out on the curb. Meatball hero and all.

Party Manners

Advanced Rules:

Greet the host and the host's parents when you get there • Have fun, or pretend to have fun • Eat and drink what's available and don't request substitutes • Go along with the program • Follow the house rules • Thank the host and the host's parents when you leave

When you are still taking your child to and from parties, you can at least gather some sense of what went on and how your child behaved. You can insist on thanking the hosts when you leave, and your child's interaction with the other kids tells you something about the proceedings.

But once your child gets to be ten or so, she gets even more independent. She rides her bike or takes the bus or gets a ride with somebody else. And who knows what she does at the parties she goes to? All you can do is remind her, before she sets off for the latest event on her calendar, that she should do the following:

Greet the host and the host's parents when you get there.

Adults need to know who is present so they know who they're responsible for. Your child should make himself known, especially if he hasn't met these grown-ups before. "Hi, I'm Felix, Jim's friend from baseball," would be enough identification.

Have fun, or pretend to have fun.

Complaining, either out loud or in mime, about the food, company, or entertainment at a party is the height of rudeness. A preteen has enough self-control and acting technique to smile and seem happy for a couple of hours, even if he's bored stiff.

Eat and drink what's available and don't request substitutes.

Scarlett O'Hara used to eat before parties. Very picky eaters or kids with allergies can do the same. Nobody wants to hear about lactose intolerance with twenty hulking twelve-year-olds to feed.

Go along with the program.

A child who hates bowling probably shouldn't go to a bowling party. Sitting in a corner refusing to participate will make everyone uncomfortable.

Follow the house rules.

This seems like an obvious point, but a group of kids can easily lose sight of household regulations. If Marina's parents don't allow sodas in the living room, Marina's guests should keep their Cokes in the kitchen. Disobeying would not only embarrass the poor girl, it would get her in trouble with her parents. ("Your friends are so rude, you're never having a party again!")

Thank the hostess and her parents when you leave.

Each guest should be sure to say "Good-bye, thank you, I had a wonderful time." Or "What a nice party." This is probably the most important rule of all, because it's those parting words that parents will remember long after the guests are gone.

Thank-You Notes

Mention something you appreciate about the gift • If it's money, say what you plan to do with it • Write a rough draft first • Don't type your note • Avoid commercial thank-you cards • Kids address their own notes • *Extra Credit: Don't start with "Thanks for the . . ."

Writing thank-you notes is never going to be fun, but by the time your children are ten, it should at least be routine. The physical act of penning a couple of coherent, courteous sentences is no longer onerous. So, of course, it's time to up the ante and make the enterprise more challenging.

The donor of a gift put time and thought and money into choosing, wrapping, and sending that gift. The author of a note must also put visible time and thought into her response. That's why we expect more of older children—more neatness, more appreciation, a longer note—and all within a week of receiving the gift. Sure, it's a lot of work, but so was going to the Gap to pick out that green sweater. A thank-you note that follows these rules is sure to impress and gratify.

Mention something you appreciate about the gift.

"It was just what I wanted" is always a good line, especially if it's true. If the donor has tried to suit your child's interests, that's very thoughtful. "I am still crazy about ballet so I will enjoy reading the book about Margot Fonteyn." Even if the gift is inappropriate, there's a way to say something nice about it. If it's too young, the phrase could be, "I have always liked board games." If it's hand-made, it could be "You must have put so much time into knitting/ crocheting/carving/modeling it." As a parent you can acknowledge to your child that a gift doesn't always hit the mark, but never denigrate the donor, and always stress the effort that went into a gift. Because that's really what you're thanking people for.

If it's money, mention what you plan to do with it.

"Dear Aunt Lisa, I've been saving up for a new video game and your gift of $10 means I'll be able to buy it a lot sooner. It's called NBA Jam. Next time you visit maybe I can show it to you. Love, Tony." This fosters a sense of connection, even if Aunt Lisa doesn't know what the NBA is.

Write a rough draft first.

By fifth grade, kids have gotten to the point where presentation counts. They have to copy over—or type—reports for school. Era-sures and crossing out are no longer acceptable to teachers, and they shouldn't be in correspondence either. Sending a note that's full of mistakes looks as if you didn't care enough to write it neatly. Clean copies should also be written in pen rather than pencil, on good stationery or note cards. Parents, by the way, should probably read over the rough drafts for spelling errors. I heard a story not long ago about a boy who thanked his grandmother for a "moron" sweater and she was a little annoyed until she realized he meant "maroon."

Don't type your note.

This is a rule that may well change by the time our children are grown, but for the moment, typed thank-you notes look cold and uncaring. I think an exception could be made for a note produced on a computer art or writing program that clearly involved a lot of effort, if it was addressed to someone who will discern that (in other words, probably not to a grandparent). It should still be signed by hand.

Avoid commercial thank-you cards.

I'm straying into the area of taste here. But remember, the general idea is that it should look as if time and effort have gone into writing a note. Handing any part of the effort over to a commercial concern like Hallmark is shirking the task.

Kids address their own notes.

Parents may have to provide the address (or simply provide an address book into which your child copies all the addresses she'll need). And, of course, the postage.

*Extra credit: Don't start with "Thanks for the. . . ."

This is tricky even for grown-ups, but it makes a note more graceful and charming if your child (or you) can back into the real reason for the letter. Alternative openings might be something like: "You are always so kind to think of me. . . ." "I was so happy to hear from you this Hanukkah. . . ." "I had a wonderful birthday this year. Dad took us to the Ice Capades and the next day, your gift arrived in the mail. . . ."

At the risk of sounding like a broken record, let me reiterate that children who produce pleasant thank-you notes will create a wonderful impression. Maybe it's unusual to see such courtesy in children, but what a great way for your kids to stand out!

Good Housemates

A s children get older, they get bigger. Obvious, right? And
as they get bigger, they take up more room in your house.
And their possessions get bigger, too. Bigger shoes, bulkier
backpacks, fatter books. And although you may once have
thought that no creatures required more equipment than a newborn,
that was only because your baby wasn't playing ice hockey yet.

In other words, as your children reach the preteen years, they
start to become large, emphatic presences in your home, and it is all
the more important that they be housebroken. (Especially because in
the next few years they will only get larger, and possibly hostile.)
In Part II, I spelled out some of the habits of a good housemate.
Here are some additional considerate customs that will make your
ever-growing children a lot easier to live with, now and in the
future.

Hang up wet towels.

Grown-ups know that wet towels start to smell after a while.
Kids need to learn this. My mother-in-law once spent an entire
week at college with Rick, using a smelly towel, and she never

complained because that would have been rude to her host (otherwise known as her negligent son). He's never forgotten that lesson, but I'm not willing to use smelly towels when I visit *my* sons at school. Hence the reminder to hang the towels where they belong, and maybe hooks specially mounted a bit lower than usual to make this possible.

Wring out and hang up wet washcloths.

They start to smell *really* fast. You can use a two-pronged approach here. On the one hand, show your child how to grab the washcloth in both hands and twist the ends in different directions to squeeze out all the water, and demonstrate just where the washcloth should be hung up. And issue reminders. When you begin to feel that you aren't being heard any more, omit the reminders and let the washcloth sit moistly in the tub. Until it smells. At which point your child will complain and you can say, "Well, honey, that's what happens when you don't wring it out." Repeat as often as necessary.

Take your hair out of the bathtub drain and throw it away.

Especially urgent with girls. A friend of mine, one of five sisters, is amazingly adept at whipping the trap out of a drain and removing the collected hairball, but it would be nicer if things never got to that point. In reality the average preteen girl has many other things to think of in the bathroom besides her hair clogging the drain, and she'll stay in there for ages without *dreaming* of cleaning up after herself. But that doesn't mean she should get away with it. Introduce her to the concept of the clogged drain. Let her know how much the plumber charges per hour. Or demonstrate the technique for unclogging the drain, and show her the hair that is mostly her color, matted like seaweed on the trap. And be prepared to nag.

If you break something, take responsibility.

You wouldn't want your twelve-year-old trying to glue the handle back on Granny's best teapot. But you would want her to own up that she broke it, and offer an apology. This is *not* an occasion for nagging: Kids feel terrible when they've done damage, and often they'll imagine exaggerated consequences. Into the panic that follows the tinkling of broken glass, you can sow calm. Let your child do most of the picking up and help with the repair, if there is any to be done. Then don't mention it again. This calm, practical approach to damage is the best way to foster a responsible attitude on your child's part, too. If the damage is done to property that belongs to someone outside the family, an offer of repair or restitution is also essential.

If you eat the last of something, put it on the shopping list.

There is nothing more irritating than reaching into the freezer to put away the frozen peas, and realizing that there's no more ice cream. (Actually, it would be worse to reach in late at night and pull out an empty ice cream carton, but I can't *imagine* who puts empty cartons back in the freezer.) Anyone in the house who can both eat and write should avoid shortages by adding to the shopping list, which, to make things easy, should be near the refrigerator.

But while grown-ups might peel the last carrot or empty that box of baking soda, preteens are more likely to scarf the last chocolate chip cookie or tortilla chip. Nonnecessities. So you can make your point by simply not buying those extras that aren't on the shopping list. You come home, you unpack the groceries, your daughter wails when she see there's no caffeine-free diet Coke. At which point you say innocently, "But it wasn't on the shopping list!" She'll learn.

Refill the ice trays.

If you have an ice-making machine you can skip this. If you don't, you know how annoying it is to reach into the ice bin, find no ice, pull out the ice trays, and find one lonely cube nestled in solitary splendor at the end. When I was growing up, our refrigerator had a big message drawn in magic marker at the bottom of the freezer: REFILL ICE TRAYS! I'm not sure it helped. But it's one way to get the point across. You might also try a brief lecture about cooperation and living together with respect for the rest of the family, and how using up all the ice cubes without refilling the trays is selfish and inconsiderate. Allow yourself to be slightly ridiculous about this: Permit your children a laugh at your expense. "Oh, Mom and her ice trays!" They won't forgot them, though.

Don't put wet things on polished wood.

In order words, a bathing suit wrapped up in a beach towel does not belong on mahogany. It really belongs hung up somewhere to dry, but if it is going to be rested momentarily anywhere, it shouldn't be on a wood surface. I'm not sure this is really manners, but I'm always astonished that men, grown men like my husband, don't know that you don't hang a sweater to dry on the back of a wooden chair. And if a mom doesn't point this out, who will?

If you work hard on these rules you might be able to make them habit by the time your children hit their teens. They'll probably vanish entirely while your kids are in college, since dorm living really *needs* to be squalid. But they'll probably emerge once again in adult life, and you'll be able to pride yourself on having reared that rare creature, a considerate roommate.

Computer Courtesy

Advanced Rules:

Be careful about installing new programs • Check for viruses • Restore default values • Don't use all capital letters when you're writing online • Keep your language clean online • Don't be a smart aleck online

Younger children are more likely to need some help with the computer, which gives a parent the chance to monitor the goings-on. And once you've laid the ground rules banning food and drink and sloppiness, the average seven-year-old can't get into too much trouble playing Where in the World is Carmen Sandiego? It's when they start exploring other capabilities of the computer that older children need a few more rules. For instance:

Be careful about installing new programs.

One day in the lunchroom Jeremy and Gabriel get to talking about how much fun Oregon Trail is. Gabriel says, "Hey, I'll lend you the disks." Jeremy comes home with three disks in his backpack, sits down at the computer and types INSTALL. The whole system comes crashing down. And of course it would be the day when Mom has to do the monthly bookkeeping for her business. Bruce Stark, of The Computer Tutor in New York, points out that only somebody who really knows what she's doing—or is willing to read the manual—should install programs.

Check for viruses.

Yes, they're really out there. This is not some paranoid fantasy, as those who've seen their data start melting away can tell you. If you're going to load a disk from your computer into somebody else's machine, run it through the virus checker first. By the same token, be careful about importing viruses. If your child brings a disk home from a friend's, for instance, he should run it through the virus checker there before he leaves. Failing to take these steps is a little like sending your child to school when you know he's coming down with chicken pox. Maybe it's not what we conventionally think of as "manners," but taking precautions to avoid the spread of disease (in humans or computers) is real courtesy.

Restore default value.

Say Vanessa had a paper due, but it wasn't quite as long as her teacher wanted it. Say Vanessa was a computer whiz and realized that she could type her paper in a slightly larger typeface than usual, and maybe her teacher would be fooled. Say Vanessa left the word processing application set to print everything in 14-point type. Somebody's going to be pretty peeved when the pages of his report come hissing out of the printer just a little bit too big. Some kids will be meticulous about this but most will need reminding until their college roommates take over the job for you. Point out that resetting the default values is as basic as putting the milk back in the refrigerator.

Don't use all capital letters when you're writing online.

On the big commercial online services (CompuServe, Prodigy, and America Online) there are lots of news groups, bulletin boards, and chat rooms geared toward kids. To participate, kids type their comments or questions, which are then sent by the computer, and responses appear on the screen. Online etiquette is pretty simple so far, but one peculiarity is that you don't type in capital letters: That's the equivalent of shouting at someone.

Keep your language clean online.

Epithets and slang that might slip by unnoticed out loud look quite shocking in black and white on your computer monitor. What's more, the kids' areas of the commercial services are carefully monitored to keep things strictly G-rated. But maybe what's most important is that the world of online communication is just taking shape, and most responsible people want to make sure that it's wholesome.

Don't be a smart aleck online.

That know-it-all stance that's so irritating in mere conversation has even more impact online. And there's not much tolerance for that kind of showing off. You risk getting "flamed" (scolded in very strong words). Better to save witticisms for the schoolyard.

I don't have any doubt that, in the next five years or so, communication via computer will become not only more widespread but also more complicated. Probably a whole new system of courtesy will evolve. There are already several different "smileys," or signals built from punctuation, that add an emotional spin to the words on the screen. But for the time being, these guidelines will keep your child courteous will he uses the computer.

Audience Participation

Advanced Rule:

Don't applaud between movements.

T he rules for good audience behavior don't change. Once your child understands about sitting still and not talking or eating or jangling loud jewelry, he's probably as well behaved as any adult in the auditorium. But there is one more mistake to be avoided, and children as young as ten can figure out how to skirt it.

Don't applaud between movements.

Musical movements, that is. Many musical pieces—and some dance pieces set to classical music—are divided into movements, or thematic sections. What's tricky is that an orchestra will come to an absolute stop. There will be silence. But the thing isn't over yet. In all but the most sophisticated audiences, somebody usually starts clapping and is then hushed up, covered with blushes. You don't want this to happen to your child. So warn her: You don't start clapping until people bow. Or until everybody else is clapping, too.

Good Sportsmanship

A child who has mastered the sportsmanship suggestions set out in Part II won't make any enemies in her competitive career. But this refinement will make her into an even better sport.

Don't blame someone or something else for your loss.

Kids as old as nine may still be so torn up by losing that they can't accept the fact that they personally blew it. So they blame the pitcher, or their mitt, or the uneven ground next to third base. Anything rather than taking responsibility. Older children, though, understand that everybody loses sometimes and it doesn't mean they're terrible athletes or chess players. They should be able to accept a loss without trying to lay the blame somewhere else. Remember Tonya Harding and her broken skate lace? That sure didn't win her any friends. If you catch your child in this tendency, gently point out that even if it really was the umpire's fault, it's better manners not to complain. (A legitimate complaint can be pursued in a calmer frame of mind, of course.) Better to accept the loss and look forward to the next time.

Good Grooming

It is a traditional part of the Order of Things that parents shall nag their children about brushing their hair and teeth and cleaning their nails. Many kids love to be grubby, and even those who don't actually revel in dirt often resent the time it takes to remove it. Why should they *bother* to wash their hands and comb their hair?

I'll skip the part about germs and get straight to the part about respect. A neat and clean appearance demonstrates respect for the company you're with and the event you're attending. Showing up at the dinner table with dirt under your nails makes it look as if you don't think it was worth getting out the nail brush just to have dinner with your boring old family. (This may well be true, but it should never be expressed.) Good grooming goes hand in hand with dressing appropriately and has to be done for the same reasons. For any occasion that involves social time with adults—family meals included—children should follow these rules. Reminders will be necessary, over and over again. You can expect a lot of complaining about your ridiculous standards. The expected reply is, "When you live by yourself you can eat dinner with dirt all over your face, but you won't do it at my table."

Wash up.

Faces, hands, and any visible skin surfaces should be as clean as possible. Many kids don't seem to realize that they *own* necks, or that dirt accumulates behind the ears. Washing hands and faces before a meal, and being sent back to clean up the spots that got missed, should be part of the routine.

Shower if necessary.

Children hit puberty unbelievably early in postindustrial America. That means, among other things, B.O. You don't ever want to embarrass kids by suggesting that this is a problem, so perhaps ten minutes for a shower should routinely be built into grooming time.

Remove foreign substances.

That means gum in the mouth and junk under the nails. Also any snacks lingering in the braces.

Arrange hair.

Notice that I'm not saying "comb." That would probably be too much to ask in the era of fashionably disheveled locks. But for even the simplest family occasion, hair should look the way it's supposed to look. In other words, if your daughter comes in from soccer with her braids all sweaty and matted down, she should brush and rebraid her hair before she joins the family.

Sit up straight.

As bodies change, kids slouch. Growth is so fast that they may not yet have a clear sense of just where their feet end. Girls may hunch over to hide emerging breasts. Parents can't really stop this, but they can insist that at meals, spines should not curl over into a C.

In conservative communities, grooming standards might be more strict: short hair on boys, smooth hair on girls, no makeup, no pierced anything. But the most important point is that your children should look *clean*.

Stranger Anxiety

Answer any questions briefly • Be prepared to move away.

D

on't talk to strangers. Be polite and answer grown-ups' questions. On the one hand, safety, on the other good manners. Is it all right for your child to chat with a pleasant-looking woman on the bus? How about a pleasant-looking man on the bus? Can you trust your child's judgment about "pleasant-looking?" What should she do if somebody asks her for the time?

The answers to these questions depend on your child's character, your local community, and your own sense of caution. You may even loosen or tighten your guidelines in response to external events or a new demonstration of your child's maturity. Safety must always be our first priority, closely followed by our children's sense of security in the larger world. Courtesy is a distant third. But, as every southern belle knows, there are still polite ways to give someone the brush-off.

Rick and I haven't yet introduced these rules to our children because the boys are still young enough to be accompanied by adults all the time. If someone whose looks I don't like tries to strike up a conversation, I'll move my sons out of reach. But I have to point out that, aside from outright nut cases, most of the strangers who want to talk to small, obviously chaperoned children are benign, so I frequently don't interfere.

It's people who want to talk to unaccompanied kids that are more worrisome. A few weeks ago I had just finished inline skating in the park and I sat on a bench to take off my skates. There was a girl sitting at the other end of the bench, adjusting her skates, while her father was already gliding around, about twenty yards away. I started to chat with her as I unlaced and unbuckled and peeled off my knee pads. Before I had all the stuff off, her father was back, hovering. And I couldn't blame him. His little girl probably shouldn't have talked to me. The sad fact is that well-meaning adults who get a polite dismissal from kids will be understanding. They know why children have to be so careful.

If you want to be sure your children can courteously halt a conversation with someone they don't know, explain the following rules. You might also want to role-play with them: There's nothing like practice to make a potentially tense situation seem more manageable.

Answer any questions briefly.

Some questions—"What time is it?" "Which way is uptown?" "Is it raining outside?"—can be answered with a couple of words. A terse reply signals to the innocent inquirer that this is a cautious child who should be left alone. Questions with more complex answers, like requests for directions, should be answered, "I don't know." The message your child conveys is, "I am being polite, but I do not want to talk to you." The girl with the inline skates was probably too forthcoming: I wouldn't have gone on chatting with her if she hadn't said, "We have the same kind of knee pads, don't we?" On the other hand, there was her dad not far away, six foot seven in his inline skates, so she obviously felt safe.

Be prepared to move away.

Innocent strangers who are attuned to the threats kids face these days won't press on with a conversation. Some people will. Maybe they're rash or maybe they're drunk or maybe they're somebody to really worry about. So at any sign of persistence, your child should move away. Change seats on a bus, change cars on a train, hop back on her bike and pedal off. No harmless adult will follow.

* * *

It's a pity we have to teach our children to be so careful, but those are the conditions of life these days. And I suppose we do run the risk that our children may offend some well-intentioned adults by being so brusque and incommunicative. But better rude and safe than polite and sorry.

Tinsel Teeth

The Basic Rules:

Keep the tools in your mouth or out of sight • Don't
pick in public • Keep your braces clean

I had braces for seven years, and my mouth was a proving ground
for all kinds of orthodontic techniques, including rubber bands.
At one point, there were five of the things strung from upper
to lower jaw, including one that made a triangle right at the
front of my mouth. Naturally I couldn't eat or drink or talk or even
think with these things in place so I frequently took them out. Also,
they often broke, and I had to remove the dangling remains.

It drove my mother nuts that I left these damp little rubber circles
scattered all over the house, and I could never understand why. I
mean, my sister's retainer had cost a hundred dollars so we could
see why it annoyed Mom that it got tangled up in the vacuum
cleaner. (It was also an expensive call to the Electrolux repairman.)
But a few rubber bands here and there seemed like a real non-
issue. Now, of course, my sympathy is with Mom. Stuff that comes
out of anybody's mouth should never see the light of day for longer
than it takes to reach a wastebasket.

Having braces is no fun for anybody, not for the poor victim
who wears them and not for the poor parent who has to pay for
and live with them. This period of life can be made easier if the
wearer of braces remembers the following suggestions.

Keep the tools in your mouth or out of sight.

Some of my friends could do amazing tricks with their retainers,
flicking them out of their mouths and flipping them around in the

air. Teachers always thought this was gross, which was probably why we did it. Teacher-baiting aside, your child might be more discreet if you provided her with a box to keep retainer, rubber bands, and night brace together in one place, preferably in her room. This certainly doesn't guarantee compliance, but it may make it easier.

Don't pick in public.

When the surfaces of your teeth are textured like a steel cheese grater, stuff is going to get stuck in them. And of course anything in your mouth feels six times larger than life. That doesn't mean it should be immediately excavated with the fingers, though. Point out the efficiency of consolidating the picking sessions right after meals, in front of a mirror, with a good strong light and a firm-bristled toothbrush.

Keep your braces clean.

From a purely aesthetic point of view, a mouth festooned with spinach is unattractive. You don't even have to lecture your child about hygiene or the possibility of cavities if you can somehow very delicately hint that keeping braces pristine is a way to minimize their visual impact. If you've ever visited the oral hygiene area of your drugstore you'll realize that American ingenuity has concocted amazing tools to keep mouths clean. Ask your child's orthodontist for guidance and invest in some specially tufted brushes and floss threaders.

Orthodontia is one of the tedious features of prepubescence, but with a little effort the aesthetic downside of the braces can be eliminated, restricting the nuisance factor to discomfort and cost.

Tuning Out

Advanced Rules:

The dinner hour is sacred • Don't try to participate in a conversation when you're wearing earphones • Silence is golden

A friend of mine who grew up in the South remembers being reprimanded at age nine or ten for reading a book while he was in the company of grown-ups doing that mysterious grown-up activity, sitting around and chatting. He couldn't figure out at the time how he was bothering anyone.

Not many adults nowadays are going to get on any child's case for *reading*. But preteens and teenagers are still almost indecently eager to escape adult company in any way they can. Actually, I don't think kids should have to feign interest in adult conversation. There's nothing wrong with escaping into a CD or playing with a video game when there are no more entertaining options. What's more, grown-ups can talk longer and more freely when they don't have to consider the interests or discretion of a preadolescent. But there are some limits on the settings or uses of escape.

The dinner hour is sacred.

Or whatever meal it is that your family gathers at. The whole point is for family members to focus on each other, and this is sterling training for the social skills. Sulky, unwilling, monosyllabic kids should come to the table without props or distractions.

Don't try to participate in a conversation when you're wearing earphones.

Some kids are such eager beavers that they just can't bear to miss anything. These are the ones who, even through their headphones, attempt to follow conversations and pitch in their own two cents' worth from time to time—at excessive volume. You can't fault their enthusiasm, but you can point out that they need to choose between music and speech. Be tactful. Self-consciousness always lurks close to the surface at this age, and if you point out that they're talking too loudly, they may stop talking completely.

Silence is golden.

Face it, part of the fun of hand-held video games is the noise they make. That doesn't mean you have to like it, but a little give-and-take on the limits here would be wise. There's nothing wrong with letting your child know you don't like the noise. But if your choice is having your child keep you company in the kitchen, beeping, or exiling child and machine to a far corner of the house, wouldn't it be nicer to have the company? On the other hand, some of these machines can be silenced and you and your child can work out, together, when and where the sound effects are acceptable. You may have to yield something in this bargain, and in fact it would be only fair. You're likely to get better compliance if something that drives your child nuts—Mozart? the vacuum cleaner?—is limited.

When you're laying down limits on tuning out, be sure you also spell out when it's perfectly okay. This is just a negotiating tool. No, you may not bring your Game Boy to Grandma's birthday party, but you can use it in the car, in your room, with your pals, on the way to school. Be sure to stress how much freedom your child has. It will make the limitations seem less significant.

Young Romance

No PDA • Don't tie up the phone • Don't tie up the computer • Take it easy on the gifts • Be nice

Today's children are terrifyingly precocious, and one symptom of that precocity is the age at which they start to date. If you're lucky, your children will be well into their teens before you have to face this issue, but some kids will be paired off as early as eleven. If yours is one of these, buckle your seat belt.

Some of these relationships are actually very innocent. The mother of one fifth-grader I know said she could never figure out why Lila was her son Ned's girlfriend, rather than just friend. Apparently sex had nothing to do with it: Lila and Ned had simply decided they were dating. What this meant in practical terms was frequent phone calls and family dinners at each other's houses. On the other hand, my friend Diane was at her wit's end trying to chaperone her eleven-year-old son and his ten-year-old girlfriend, who apparently spent most of their "study sessions" necking.

So where do manners come in here? Courtesy to the mate, for one thing. Courtesy to the rest of us who aren't blissfully in love, for another. And consideration for the family that still has to coexist with the lovebird. In practical terms, you will want to bring up the following guidelines.

No PDA.

That stands for "public display of affection." Kissing, hugging, nuzzling, whatever. Nothing makes an onlooker more uncomfortable. You can't control what your child does with his main squeeze, but you can insist that it be kept private.

But how do you enforce this rule? That's going to depend in large part on your kids. The secretive ones will never betray by as much as a glance that they have done their bit to explore the prepubescent libido. Other, more exhibitionistic kids will drape themselves all over each other at the front door just as everybody's trying to get out of the house. You can always try a tactful approach by having a private discussion with your young lover and simply saying that affection needs to be more discreet. If there isn't any improvement, brisk reminders are probably in order.

Don't tie up the phone.

Teenagers in love will linger on the phone for hours, just listening to each other breathe. Preteens, since they're still really children, can be even sillier, but you don't have to let them. The telephone is installed as a convenience to the entire family and must not be monopolized. Feel free to set a limit to the length of phone calls. Who's paying the bill, anyway? Point out, if your children haven't already, that the letters MOM actually stand for "Mean Old Mom."

Don't tie up the computer.

If both parties have computers and belong to online services, they could very easily spend long hours sending each other inconsequential e-mail or even "chatting." This is hard to police since so many kids do homework on computers, but you can always threaten to cut off the online service if the bills exceed a certain amount.

Take it easy on the gifts.

It's human nature to want to lay tribute at the loved one's feet. Given the ephemeral nature of juvenile romances, though, the tribute shouldn't be very substantial. In Victorian times a girl could only accept flowers, candy, or books from a suitor, and it would be nice to have a rule like that today. If presents have to be purchased out of your child's allowance, they won't be too lavish. But most kids also have to be warned not to give away things that *they've* been given. My friend Sophie was very hurt when she saw a ring that she'd given her son, Todd, on a chain around Todd's girlfriend's neck.

Be nice.

You'd think this point would be obvious. but part of what's going on when preteens get involved in romance is the same kind of role-playing and examination of identity that preoccupies them in all their waking hours. "Am I a love-them-and-leave-them type?" or "What would happen if I flirted with Sam's best friend?" As a parent you need to establish that a boyfriend or girlfriend should be treated politely, just like friends, family members, and new acquaintances. Consistent courtesy to *your* mate is the first step here. Other than that, you can model good manners toward the loved one: "Do you think George would like to come hiking with us?" "Does Elizabeth need any help getting around with her ankle in that cast?" And if you spot lack of consideration, it's time for a little lecture. Your child might be surprisingly receptive to it, because he's in the middle of trying to figure out how this whole dating thing works. You're offering a tool that may help it work better.

Early ventures into romance tend to be intense, and your child may be completely preoccupied by what Cupid's arrows have done to him. Nevertheless, he lives in a family and a community, and he can't be permitted to neglect courtesy to everyone he comes in contact with. Least of all the Loved One.

• COURTLY GESTURES •

I support unisex manners. I don't see why a woman shouldn't help a man put on his coat and I think the person who holds the door should be the one who gets there first. So I am ambivalent about a couple of holdover habits, courteous gestures that might make a woman feel cherished—or might annoy the daylights out of her. I'd hate to see them die out, but I'm not sure they belong in the twenty-first century. So I'll leave that to you. If you think your twelve-year-old son has the makings of a Fred Astaire, these habits will suit him.

Gentlemen walk on the outside of the sidewalk.

Hundreds of years ago, men accompanying ladies took care to walk on the street-ward side of the damsel. This protected women from the mud of the streets and from unsavory substances being tossed out overhanging windows. And possibly from attack by highwaymen. The custom clearly serves no practical purpose nowadays, but it does express consideration for female frailty.

Gentlemen rise when a lady enters the room.

My husband belonged to a very stuffy all-male club when we were in college. Whenever I went there for dinner, all of the boys would stand up when I sat down at the table. I have to say, it made me feel wonderful. Even so, I'm reluctant to suggest that boys stand up for a woman but not for a man: I'd rather see them rise for all adults. (See Rise and Shine, page 140.) Still, the tradition exists, and a lot of women are flattered to see a man leap to his feet in their presence.

A gentleman holds a lady's chair as she seats herself at the table.

Women, fragile creatures that they are, might not be strong enough to pull in their own chairs when they sit down. The only people who regularly hold chairs for women now are captains in expensive restaurants, and the deliberately debonair. But a boy who holds his grandmother's chair at Thanksgiving dinner might completely charm her.

PART IV

For Parents Only

The basic premise of this book is that children aren't going to have good manners unless their parents put some effort into teaching them. I've realized, though, as I worked my way through it, that our job in teaching courtesy is more than just describing the behavior we want and then nagging until it's a habit. One of the most important parts of the entire project, and one that falls wholly to us grown-ups, is *making it possible* for our children to be polite.

My husband's cousin has raised four remarkably nice children. So when I started working on this book I called Pat to see what her philosophy was. She said, "The most important thing is, first, to make sure your kids know what to expect in a given situation. And second, don't ask more of them than they can handle. Don't ask a three-year-old to sit through a church service without some books to look at. And don't ask a six-year-old to write perfect thank-you notes. Always make sure your kids know how you want them to act, and be sure they're able to do it."

I think that's great advice. But I'd take it further. Sometimes we can do things ourselves to make good manners easier for children. First, we can behave in a way that brings out *their* best behavior, by being as courteous and patient with them as possible. Second, we can sometimes control the situations we put our kids in, to make them easier to handle.

So that's what's in this section. This is not the part of the book where you learn how to take the bones out of a quail or how to address a four-star general. (Sorry, I know that's what you really wanted.) It's the part where I tell you what *you* need to do to help your child have good manners. It's about laying the groundwork, and having realistic expectations, so you can help your child succeed. Not all of these sections have rules, because some circumstances are too complicated for rules. Where I have used rules, they don't indicate expectations about *your* behavior as much as tips for encouraging good manners in your child. And remember, if she looks good, you look good, too.

Meeting Children

I wrote in Part I about the general confusion surrounding what children should call adults who aren't their parents. (Maybe you aren't confused; if not, you're very lucky.) Parents have a dual responsibility on the name issue. On the one hand, they have to decide what their children will call grown-ups. On the other hand, they have to decide what children will call *them*. (That means you.) And then they have to let kids know what name to use.

Are you going to be a friendly first-name type? Or would you prefer to keep a little formality in your relationship with your child's pals? Would you be the only parent in your neighborhood whom the children called "Linda?" Or the only one known as "Mrs. Rogers?" And do you care?

Once you've made your decision, you put it into practice. When you meet a child for the first time, you say, "Hi, I'm Mrs. Smith, Zerelda's mother." Or "Hi, I'm Anne." The point is, you're doing the child a favor by making it clear what name you prefer.

If the child gets it wrong, correct him. You may feel a little awkward saying, "I'd really rather be called Mrs. Smith," but you should go ahead and spit it out. Give the child every chance to get your name right, rather than letting him irritate you every time he calls you "Anne." He won't know any better unless *you* tell him.

Mealtimes

Eat regular meals together • Turn off the TV, turn
down the music • Turn on the answering machine

Each part of this book has a hefty section on table manners, because eating politely is one of the most complicated and least natural sets of skills children need to master. But it's not quite enough, and there is more for parents to do: We have to provide the setting that will make the children's learning possible. This is how.

Eat regular meals together.

I know that schedules are extremely complicated and that the days of the nuclear family seated around the table at 6:30 every night are a thing of the past. Still, you can't teach children table manners unless you're sitting at the table with them. And they'll never absorb the notion that meals are a social time unless you use them that way. At least a couple of times a week (the more the merrier, of course), the family should have meals together. Maybe this will be breakfast on the weekend. Or maybe it will be Friday night, and you'll get take-out food. That it happens at all is what matters.

Turn off the TV, turn down the music.

The point is that families should be dependent on each other for entertainment during family meals. If you're having trouble getting a conversation started, ask each person to say what was best about his day. There's nothing like enthusiasm to break the conversational ice.

Turn on the answering machine.

If you've gone to all that trouble to carve out family time, why let the Little League coach interrupt it? Let the machine catch the calls and turn down the volume to eliminate any temptation to pick up the phone.

Helping your children appreciate that mealtimes are as much about communication as they are about eating is the first step to instilling good table manners.

• B O O K W O R M •

Have you ever noticed the hush that falls at a birthday party when the cake is served? Little kids don't naturally associate eating with talking. They eat with concentration, then the noise resumes. Not until they're older do they really appreciate meals as social times, opportunities to exchange information or to get to know people or to argue heatedly about the playoffs.

Social mealtimes are important. So are books, though. We need to encourage our children to read—but they should not read at the table. People come before books (except at breakfast, when many people aren't fully human).

I have taken Timothy out to dinner at a local coffee shop a couple of times recently. Just the two of us, out on a date. He's five. His conversation is not always fascinating, and there are these long silences while he concentrates on the French fries. The second time we went out together I slipped a paperback into my pocket, thinking there was no reason to stare into space while Timo communed with his dinner. I could read. But when I slid the book out onto my lap, I felt awkward. It seemed rude. I felt that I was subtly conveying to Timo that his company was not all that interesting. So when he caught on to what I was doing and said, "No reading at the table, Mommy," I wasn't all that sorry. He was right. No reading at the table.

Privacy

It happened when Willy turned six. All of a sudden, I couldn't come into the bathroom when he was taking a bath. "I need privacy!" he'd yell. Naturally, whatever Willy needed his little brother also needed. So Timo would shout, "I need privacy!" and then trot into the kitchen stark naked.

The thing is, at a certain point, children do need privacy. And so do their parents. So do their friends, for that matter. And probably the best way to help your children understand the notion is by respecting their privacy (however erratically they may define it) and by gently pointing out to them what you consider private. Some areas to consider:

- **Physical privacy**. At a certain point, you will no longer feel comfortable undressing around this creature who was once part of your flesh. He will arrive at this point, too, on his own timetable. This is why we have doors—so they can be closed.

- **Private possessions**. I don't like having the children go through my desk drawers, even though they aren't going to find anything more exciting than a supply of AA batteries and several chains of paper clips. Eventually, their desk and bureau drawers will be off limits to me. As should the drawers of any of their friends, or their friends' parents. The only time it's really okay to look in drawers that aren't yours is at a hotel, or with specific permission. I gather, from my friends who have daughters, that girls tend to go through their mothers' drawers. I believe this, because I still do it to my mother (and try on all her new makeup, too). I honestly don't think you can stop daughters from doing this because their investigations are part of forming a gender identity. Seriously. I mean, why else are they so intrigued by your panty hose? On the other hand, you do need your privacy, so daughters should at least ask permission before checking out the contents of your closet, drawers, or purse.

- **Telephone conversations**. Even a three-year-old isn't allowed to listen in on an extension, unless you're having a conference call. It is also not really courteous to say, when somebody hangs up the phone, "Who was that? What did she want?" although spouses sometimes tolerate this excessive curiosity. As a parent you do have to review logistical arrangements your child may make on the phone, but you don't have any right to inquire what her friend, Davina, thinks about the cute new boy in sixth grade. (Of course, if you can't figure this out from what she lets drop, you need a little course in intelligence-gathering.)

- **Written material**. I go through Willy's backpack every day after school to retrieve notices sent home to me. I read his homework notebook so I know what the evening's assignment is. This feels slightly invasive and before long I will have to stop. The basic rule here is that nobody should read anybody else's written matter unless invited to. Not mail, not files (on paper or a computer), not first drafts of a novel hidden in the sock drawer. Certainly not a journal. You will also have to be explicit with your child about the expectation that these things are private. And as insurance, keep anything really private out of sight and out of reach.

Fine Dining

The youngest child should be able to stay seated for
at least fifteen minutes • Be sure your children can
eat fairly neatly • For a very formal restaurant, prepare your children in advance • Scale down your
expectations • Help your child with the menu • Don't
make a fuss about how much your child eats • Tip
heavily

Every now and then a family gets the idea that it would be
nice to have a meal out in a more formal restaurant, a place
where there's a candle instead of crayons on the table. This
happened to us a few years ago, when our children were five
and two; my husband decided to take Mommy out for dinner on
Mother's Day. The easiest choice was a restaurant just a block away
in our slightly funky neighborhood. The management wouldn't be
horrified by the presence of children, and the food and atmosphere
were quite festive. And I wouldn't have to wash the dishes.

Well, the service was terrible. Nobody took our order for about
fifteen minutes and then half of it got lost in the kitchen. The
children, needless to say, got progressively antsy and whiny. After
several long strolls outside, Rick looked at me and said, "Honey, I
just have to take the boys home. They're starving." So I ate Mother's
Day dinner alone. (I didn't have to wash the dishes, though.)

We didn't try the restaurant experience for another two years,
and it went better, but we were with my parents-in-law. That meant
four adults to two children, which seems to be just about the right
ratio. One to take a child to the bathroom, another to cut the
spaghetti,and two to talk to each other and have a nice time. Even
so, it was not exactly relaxing.

Eating in restaurants is a lovely, civilized practice, but it's not very civilized with small children. If you'd like to make a habit of it, keep the following principles in mind. They're geared toward the very youngest children, because the little ones have the hardest time with the atmosphere in a formal restaurant. Remember the phrase, "You can dress him up but you can't take him out." I'm sure it was coined to describe a four-year-old.

The youngest child should be able to stay seated for at least fifteen minutes.

I don't have a lot of patience with parents who let their children wander around and "make friends" at restaurants. Some of the customers are shelling out good money to baby-sitters just to get away from the younger set. On the other hand, the pace of restaurant eating can be difficult for a preschooler. At home, you sit down and the food is on the table. It's hard for a three-year-old to decide on the ravioli and then wait ten minutes (an eternity) for it to arrive. So one of the adults simply must be prepared to take long walks to the parking lot and the bathroom and other local features of interest.

It will also help to have a few quiet diversions in your bag. The food, when it does arrive, will keep a child busy for only a few minutes. Just as you are finally getting your fish boned, your daughter will be done with her chicken and ready for more fun. A couple of slender books and a handful of play figures could buy you several peaceful bites.

Be sure your children can eat fairly neatly.

When Timo was two I took him to a Chinese restaurant and foolishly picked up the chopsticks when the food came. He naturally enough insisted on trying to eat his meal—rice, of course—with chopsticks. By the time we left it looked as if our table had suffered a highly localized blizzard, and I've never dared to go back. I'm not saying your child has to be able to get every pea on the plate, but some skill is essential, not only to simplify cleanup but so that neighboring diners aren't shocked.

For a very formal restaurant, prepare your children in advance.

My oldest friend has four sons and she recently had to leave her family for a week. Her husband decided, in her absence, to take the boys to Sunday brunch at the local country club, a very dressy and stuffy place. He actually ran a rehearsal at home: got the boys all dressed up, served them breakfast, and had them critique each other's manners after the meal. The actual meal at the club went like clockwork, and when Lisa got home, all she heard about for days was the sight of her menfolk out on the town, behaving beautifully. You may not want to go this far, but you can certainly describe a restaurant ahead, guess what might be on the menu, and point out that the pace will be slower than dinner at home.

Scale down your expectations.

Forget lingering over coffee. Skip hors d'oeuvres unless your kids are old hands at restaurant dining. Sitting and chatting and admiring food is just not appealing to them, and the novelty of the surroundings wears off after about half an hour. Still, you can have fun if you order one course, make sure your salad comes with your main course, and order the most outrageous dessert available (in flames, if possible).

Help your child with the menu.

Steer her toward something you're pretty sure she'll like. This is no time for experimenting with new foods.

Don't make a fuss about how much your child eats.

We sometimes have to have a bowl of cereal at home after eating out. For one thing, the strange setting is often distracting, and then, things don't taste the same as they do at home. Adults may consider this an advantage, but kids (innately conservative) do not. Making a fuss will only spoil your meal, and everyone else's around you.

Tip heavily.

Kids at restaurant tables mean more work for the serving people. Your tip should acknowledge this.

Restaurant meals can be a lot of fun for the family. And they'll be a lot more fun if everyone's manners are up to snuff.

Telephone Manners

Distract a preschooler • Let an older child write you
a note • Offer to call back

I've spent a lot of time in the other chapters talking about use
of the telephone, and I'm not quite done yet. The reason there
are so many rules is that only one person in your family can use
the phone at a time, so numerous courtesies surround sharing it.
And we use the phone to make contact with other human beings,
so we also need to be polite to the people on the other end.

One of the hardest things kids have to learn early on is not so
much sharing the phone with parents, as sharing parents with the
phone. From infancy on up, they'll see it as direct competition. That
thing attached to Mom's ear has the sinister effect of diluting her
attention. She can't listen to a song or find Cookie Monster's missing
eye when she's hooked up to it. It's a threat, and calls for desperate
measures. Insistent tones. Jumping up and down. Screaming might
work. Maybe that long curly string would go around your neck?
Aha! That got her.

We've all heard parents of teenagers shouting in exasperation,
"Can't you see that I'm on the phone?" so this clearly is not an issue
that will go away once your child is six. My theory is that kids don't
really *look* at us most of the time, so when they wander into the
kitchen and say, "Mom, where's the pencil sharpener?" they simply
have not absorbed the fact that you aren't free to talk to them.
What's more, the child who will patiently wait half an hour for you
to play Monopoly just *has* to tell you something right away when

you're on the phone. He's afraid he'll forget it if he has to wait until you finish. (And you know what? He will.)

Still, adults should be able to talk on the phone without interruptions for just a few minutes. And when they say, as they have to sometimes, "Honey, I can't talk to you right now, I'm on the phone," the child should wait without complaint. The length of time you can realistically expect a child to wait will lengthen as she gets older, of course. And these techniques may help.

Distract a preschooler.

Parenting magazines often recommend keeping a basket of special toys by the phone that are available only when Mom is chatting. It's a very effective ploy if you can organize it. Some kids may even be satisfied if you'll just crouch down to their level and offer a hug.

Let an older child write you a note.

You can certainly read a note from your child while you're talking, and write the response, too. This works fine for a quick exchange of information, or a request for permission to do something.

Offer to call back.

People who don't have kids are often disconcerted by the episodic nature of a phone call in which you have to keep saying, "Excuse me? What is it, Jason? No, you may not put the dinosaurs in the dryer. Honey, I'm on the *phone!*" They will be even more disconcerted if you suddenly lose it and and bellow in That Voice, "For heaven's sake! What is this thing attached to my ear?" This is particularly unfortunate if you're trying to do business. Much better to say to your caller in a controlled voice, "Excuse me, may I call you back in a moment?" and take three minutes to get the children settled in something so absorbing that they don't know you exist. (You will probably not be able to perform this feat between 5:00 and 8:00 P.M. without resorting to TV.)

And then there are the children who want to get on the phone themselves. The younger your child is, the more cautious you should be about this. Sometimes when I'm talking to a parent I can hear a toddler grabbing for the phone. The beleaguered parent will say, "Hang on, Otto wants to say hello," and there are a few moments of mumbling and maybe a breathy little voice whispering "Hello." I'm sure it's cute but the appeal is kind of lost on me. Maybe when I'm a grandmother I'll enjoy those heavy-breathers. Just don't put your child on the line with anyone who isn't a family member, except by special request. As parents we need to edit the world for our children, but we also need to edit our children for the world.

Don't Bring the Kids

One of the most complicated things about having children is figuring out how to integrate them into your life. What happens when you get invited to a dinner party: Do you bring the baby? How about that wedding: Should the kids go? They certainly couldn't get into too much trouble if you took them to the museum to see that sculpture show—could they?

Well, they could, as you know. A preschooler can't tell the difference between a Rodin and a climbing structure. (And he won't believe it when he is let in on the secret.) So many parents find their horizons contracting considerably. If they want to spend a lot of time with their children, they have to do kid things. Go to nature museums instead of art museums, on bike rides instead of to the gym, on picnics intead of to cocktail parties.

But there are some gray areas, events where kids *might* be acceptable. Big, noisy parties, for instance. And there are parents who feel their kids are so exceptional that they'll be happy to sit through the Philharmonic's performance of Mahler's Eighth Symphony.

If you take your children someplace where they aren't explicitly welcome, you put them in a terrible position. It may be hard for them to behave according to the standards of the event. The Mayor of New York seated his eight-year-old son on the podium for his 1994 inauguration. The boy, bored to tears but stimulated by all the attention he was getting, behaved outrageously, and his antics were on the front page of the paper the next day. The father's poor judgment made the child look like a spoiled brat.

Don't do this to your kid. Ask a few questions to get a feeling for a situation ahead of time. And consider leaving the children at home if:

- They'll be kept up way past their bedtime. A tired child is not a pleasant child, and the younger they are, the more true this is.

- There won't be any other kids there. In fact, if anyone says this to you directly, they might as well add, ". . . so don't bring yours."

- They'll be bored. An elderly relative of Rick's held a cocktail party last fall and insisted that we bring the children. There was no way to say no to him. So they sat restlessly in a corner of the room, reading the books I'd brought for them and ready at any moment to burst into a furious squabble for lack of anything else to do. What's more, I hardly got to talk to anyone because I was so busy keeping them out of trouble.

- They'll have to behave like grown-ups. In other words not wiggle, not interrupt, keep their voices down, listen to incredibly dull adult conversation, and not play with anything. This is a recipe for disaster.

Remember, your children can be polite only if you don't ask too much of them. This means remembering at all times that they are children. If they were actually little grown-ups, we wouldn't have to teach them anything, would we?

• TAKING KIDS TO THE OFFICE •

Every now and then our children are going to put us in an awkward situation. Maybe it will be the old baseball through the window, or a mix-up about invitations, or even the traditional loud voice saying, "Mommy, why does he have a patch over his eye? Is he a pirate?" It will take all our grown-up poise to handle the embarrassment and even so we won't be able to think back on the episode without flinching.

That's life, part of the package with children. What doesn't have to be part of the package, though, is putting our *children* in an awkward situation. And one of the most common of these is bringing the kids to the office. Here's what you need to remember. Your colleagues cannot be rude to her. They can't say, "Honey, I've got this big project to get out by five o'clock so can I catch you tomorrow?" Work tends to grind to a halt when there are kids around. So you risk straining your colleagues' good nature if you bring your kids in too often.

Lunchtime is fine. After five o'clock is fine. The dead week between Christmas and New Year's is fine. Some offices, in fact, are always pretty child-friendly. We have one friend who works at Nickelodeon and from what I gather, having a six-year-old around doesn't make a whole lot of difference.

Emergencies are different, too. Say your daughter has pinkeye. She can't go to school, you don't want to leave her alone at home, so you grab a bunch of books off the shelf and set her up in a corner of your office and she plays "Little House on the Prairie" all day. And since you're all pretending she's not there, your colleagues don't have to entertain her.

It's the state visit, when you take your child around to meet everybody in the department and they all raid their cookie drawers to offer treats, that you can't do more than about once a year. After all, the main thing people have to say to an unfamiliar child is, "My goodness, you've grown so much!" Leave enough time between visits so your colleagues can say that and mean it.

Dress Codes

When, as a childless person, I imagined the challenges of raising children, I never considered the issue of clothes. Growing up, I wore the clothes my mother made me wear: smocked gingham dresses and dreadful red sandals with buckles. I hated them, but I had no choice in the matter.

I am a pretty strict parent, but I don't exert the kind of control over my sons' wardrobes that my mother had. So Willy goes off to school sometimes wearing a knee-length tie-dyed T-shirt topped by a New York Rangers sweatshirt that's slightly too small. There are ragged holes in the knees of his formerly presentable khakis. And he is wearing one of his cherished NFL caps. Before I became a parent, I would have looked at him and thought, "How can his mother let him go out looking like that?"

How can I? Well, it's only school. And for something more formal, I can wrangle him into appropriate duds. As far as clothes go, I am still operating on the principle we all learn so thoroughly when our children are toddlers: Pick your battles.

The clothes battle does need to be fought. Dressing appropriately for different situations is part of good manners just as much as saying "Please" and "Thank you." What are you communicating when you go to a wedding dressed in your jeans? That you didn't think the event was worth changing for. On the other hand, showing up clean and scrubbed, in a tie or a party dress, demonstrates that you have gone to some trouble to look nice. Your fashion statement indicates your respect for the occasion, and for the people involved.

Not, mind you, that I underestimate the difficulty of persuading kids to wear appropriate clothes. Preschoolers are probably the worst. Clothes tend to be a big control issue for them. They'll wear only yellow, or they want to wear everything inside out. They insist on wearing the same spaghetti-stained T-shirt four days in a row. They won't dress themselves, or they insist on dressing themselves at a pace only slightly faster than the movement of an Arctic glacier. Then there's the whole fantasy issue. How do you get the Superman cape off Jamie before you go to Grandma's sixtieth birthday party?

When you're trying to persuade a preschooler to get dressed up, you have to take your time. Some kids hate surprises, and they'll flatly refuse to wear new clothes. So you have to introduce the clothes days ahead of time. Wash them. Make sure Alex sees those new khakis a couple of times as he's putting on his sweat pants. Point out the cool features: the grown-up belt, the pockets he can put treasures in. And when the time comes to get ready for the special event, get your preschooler dressed before *you* change. Better that your child show up in dress clothes that are a little the worse for wear than in casual clothes of any description.

Usually, once you get your preschooler into the outfit she protested so wildly against, she'll wear it without complaint. The battle was about getting it on—once that's past, the clothes lose their significance. This is not always true with older children. You probably won't have the same cataclysmic struggle about dressing. But an eight-year-old girl is perfectly capable of nursing her deep resentment of a new dress and saying, on the way home from a party, "I had a terrible time. My dress scratched the inside of my right elbow the whole time." (Never mind that you saw her completely engrossed by the magician for over an hour.) Comfort becomes crucial. And as elementary school kids are intensely social, peer pressure begins to play an important role. You can shop for a four-year-old by yourself, but you need to drag your older child along with you.

I deeply love shopping. One of my great regrets, now that I have kids, is that I can't indulge myself as often as I would like in the thorough perusal of *stuff* (light bulbs, high heels, it hardly matters what) that I used to adore. Shopping with my sons is torture. But I need their input if I'm going to buy clothes that they will, however reluctantly, wear. When we're choosing everyday clothes I give them some latitude and defer to their preferences. "Would you wear this?" I ask, holding up a denim shirt that I think would look adorable. "No," sniffs Will with disdain. "I only wear short-sleeve shirts, remember?" Just checking. For dress clothes, though, my word is law. "You need a blazer." "Oh, Mom, do I *have* to?" he'll whine half-heartedly. I'll let him determine which of two blazers in our price range appeals more or fits more comfortably, but we're going home with one of them, come what may. If you're taking a child shopping for a garment she's going to hate, an attitude of empathy can be helpful. "I know you don't like dresses, Lucy. The problem is that if you don't wear a dress to your aunt's wedding, it will look as if you didn't care enough to get dressed up. So we'll see what we can find that isn't too girly looking." And give your child as much choice as possible. You determine the range of acceptability, and within those parameters it's up to her.

The final factor in this eternal wardrobe struggle is style. Some children care about style more than others, and some come to it earlier than others. The herd instinct of the preteen years, though, is very likely to affect your child's approach to her clothes. When you're shopping, the conflict is no longer just about the necessity of owning and wearing certain clothes. Your child's dawning self-image is at stake.

This is very delicate ground. On the one hand, there is your knowledge of what is appropriate and what various outfits might communicate in various settings. On the other hand, there is a fledgling personality, eager to take on a new form. Negotiation is probably the safest way to resolve this conflict.

Let's say you're shopping for an outfit to wear to a cousin's bat mitzvah. Your eleven-year-old daughter falls in love with a two-piece outfit, a cropped top with palazzo pants that leave her belly button showing. She looks stunning in it. She also looks like jail bait. No way can she wear this in a temple. On the other hand, you see that the pretty wisteria-print dress with the sailor collar that you had in mind is not going to be acceptable. She has moved on. She's too old for sailor collars. So you put your choice at one end of the spectrum and her choice at the other, and try to find something in between. Your minimum requirements are that the garment have a skirt, cover her from shoulders to midthigh, and not be sheer. Her bottom line is no flowers, no pleats, no lace or bows, and definitely not pink. You probably won't like her final choice (the whole point of preteen fashion is that we grown-ups aren't supposed to like it). The older ladies at the bat mitzvah may say, "Leah is such a pretty girl, what a pity about that dress." But then, look what *they're* wearing.

I've used a female example here because the possibilities are much wider for them. With boys, I think your struggles are more likely to involve grooming: long hair, filthy nails, maybe a pierced ear. Grooming requirements for any social occasion are absolute. Everybody has to be clean. Period. If sight of a pierced ear is going to give Great-grandfather a stroke, the earring should be removed.

It's impossible to generalize about what kinds of clothes are appropriate for what occasions. The range is just too great from one community to another. The outfits that our more formal friends' kids wear to school would be appropriate church-going garb for my sons. On the other hand, my California nieces and nephews have been known to go to church in shorts and T-shirts. There are very few absolutes, with the exception of absolute negatives— clothing choices that are always a mistake.

The first is overdressing. I've lingered on the difficulty of getting kids to dress up because I think that's a very common problem. Dressing up too much, though, is an equally poor move. Party clothes are not meant for play. They also single out your child in a group, which interferes with social dynamics. The dress (or the tie, for a boy) tends to dominate preschool play and freeze school-yard give-and-take.

Fantasy costumes have much the same effect. Most preschools insist that the Power Ranger suits be left at home because they don't want a classroom full of kicking, jabbing warriors. Maybe you don't mind taking Snow White to a party instead of your daughter, but she may insist that everyone play along with her disguise. Grown-ups will not appreciate a small child who dictates the terms of their interaction.

Finally, there's the sex issue. A friend of mine deplores her eleven-year-old daughter's desperation to wear provocative clothes and makeup. Mass culture wants to turn little girls into sex objects and they, of course, are eager to comply. Is this taste or is it manners? I'm not quite sure. I do know that a ten-year-old in dangly earrings and fishnet stockings makes me very uneasy. So maybe it is manners. We want the people we come in contact with to be comfortable.

It's fairly simple to say what kids should not wear. Positive guidelines are harder to come up with, given our country's enormous variety of tastes and habits. But I think it is possible, and helpful, for families to think in terms of three levels of formality: **normal**, **better**, and **best**.

Normal would cover every day. School, play group, sports, a picnic at the park. These would be the clothes that get the most wear: shorts, T-shirts, leggings, jumpers, sweatshirts, jeans, polo shirts, khakis.

Better is a step up. These are the clothes your child would wear for the class picture, or to a birthday party, or maybe to Mom's office. They don't differ that much from the normal variety except that they're in better shape. The colors haven't faded, stains haven't set, there are no patches or frayed cuffs. Sweat pants don't make the grade. Neither do T-shirts with cartoon characters on them.

Best means top of the line, for the most formal occasions in your child's life, like weddings or family parties. These are by definition events that include grown-ups, and require that parents dress up, too. If you can manage it, kids should have at least one dressy outfit that fits and is appropriate to the season. For girls, this would be a dress or jumper or two-piece outfit that is worn with party shoes. I don't think boys under the age of six need to wear jackets and ties to be dressed up: A handsome cotton sweater with a turtleneck or polo shirt is more comfortable and doesn't look as messy when the shirt comes untucked, as it always will. I have the sense that on the West Coast, even in a conservative community, a boy could get along without a blazer or suit until he was well into his teens. On the other hand, on the East Coast, dressed-up little boys are just small versions of dressed-up grown-ups, right down to the dark socks and polished shoes.

Dressing your children appropriately for the various occasions in their lives can be a lot of trouble. It's too bad that it doesn't get easier as they get older. At least with table manners your kids are visibly acquiring some skills; arguing about clothes is a battle that only changes its form. But if you want to be courteous to the people who are kind enough to invite you to their parties or festive occasions, you just have to fight the good fight. And make sure there's film in the camera from time to time, to record how splendid your family looks.

• H A T S   O F F •

I was looking around the beach on the Fourth of July this year and about three quarters of the males there, from the age of 5 up, were wearing baseball caps. Frontward, backward, even hiked up on the head with the crown squashed down (precarious in a stiff breeze). This is by now standard gear for most males. Hats worn by adults went out in the mid-sixties, so the etiquette of taking one's hat off has lain dormant for thirty years. If your son is one of those with a baseball cap surgically attached to his head, he might be surprised to know that there are times when it's appropriate to take the darned thing off.

During the pledge of allegiance or the national anthem.

No matter what everyone else in the stadium is doing. Explain that taking off your hat is a gesture of honor to our country.

In some houses of worship.

Same principle. Doesn't matter what your religious notions are, you can't insult someone else's by leaving your hat on. Jewish men, of course, cover their heads, but a baseball cap is not the same as a yarmulke.

At the table.

To diminish the strong resemblance between the family dinner table and a fast food restaurant.

*Extra credit: in an elevator, when a lady enters.

An archaic little bit of courtesy that will be probably net your son the surprised praise of a woman who thought she'd seen the death of good manners.

When Manners Are a Must

Say "Hello" • Say "Please" • If you make their job more difficult, apologize • Say "Thank you"

Have you ever seen someone yell at a waiter or a sales clerk? It's not a pretty picture. And somehow, even though the customer may be justified in his annoyance, you never sympathize with him. You look at the guy who's yelling and you think, "What a jerk!"

Marguerite Kelly, author of *The Family Almanac*, makes this point crystal clear. A waiter earns tips, a salesperson makes a commission, so they can't just dump a bowl of soup on a boorish customer's head. Not if they want to take home that paycheck. "If you're rude to the people who hire or teach you, you take the consequences, and that's fair. But the people who work for you are depending on you for income, so you've got to be more polite to them," says Kelly.

Of course you and your children are universally courteous anyway. But it's a good idea to emphasize an extra level of politeness to the people who can't get away from you: the bank clerk, the hairdresser, the baby-sitter. You do this in two ways: by scrupulously modeling that courtesy, and by drawing your children's attention to it and eliciting empathy. Kelly says, "I always used to tell my children, let's figure out a way to be nice to the waitress, she's on her feet all day working hard, so let's be sure we don't make a mess and let's be as nice as we can."

All encounters with people in service businesses should include the following steps:

Say "Hello."

The salesperson at the local Gap Kids is an individual with a family and a personality and possibly sore feet. Look her in the eye and greet her.

Say "Please."

"Could we please see this shoe in a size five?" "I'd like a Whopper with fries, please." "Could you please tell me where to find a biography of George Washington?" You'd want people to talk to you and your children this way.

If you make their job more difficult, apologize.

If your child tries on six pairs of jeans and then decides she's only going to wear skirts, or if she spills her Coke all over the floor, she's making someone else work harder without any payoff. This should be acknowledged by the parent and pointed out to the child.

Say "Thank you."

But you knew that, didn't you?

In the House of the Lord

Be prepared to bail out • Be prepared with distractions • No snacking • Dress your children in quiet shoes • Observe sartorial customs • Ask if you're unsure about anything

Tolerance for normal childish rowdiness is probably at an all-time low on airplanes and in houses of worship. I don't have much patience with cranky air travelers, but I do feel strongly that people in synagogues and churches and mosques should be able to concentrate on their prayers.

Desirable juvenile behavior varies widely from one religious establishment to another. I heard recently about an Episcopal church in the South where, during the service, children were allowed to take their toys anywhere in the church except on the altar itself. They usually settled right up front, driving their Tonka trucks between the feet of the priest as he led the service. The rector of this church felt that children's spirituality should be allowed to develop unfettered, and the rest of the adults in the parish apparently concurred. At the other end of the spectrum is a church in Manhattan that doesn't allow children into the main service until they're twelve, capable of maintaining an adult level of decorum.

In most houses of worship, regardless of religion or denomination, you won't go wrong with the following:

Be prepared to bail out.

If you have a young child with you, don't count on staying put for the entire proceedings. Scope out the closest exit ahead, and when whispers escalate into whines or wails, quietly scoop up the child and leave. You do have some latitude here. If there are lots of children present and there's a constant rustly accompaniment to the official proceedings, you can stick it out a little longer. But a restless child will rarely calm down unless you can provide distraction. And remember: If you don't respond to a whisper, the repetition will be louder. Even if your child has barely zipped up his pants from the last trip, it's unwise to ignore a request to go to the bathroom, because before you know it that request will be made at the top of your child's lungs. During silent prayer, of course.

Be prepared with distractions.

Some child-friendly churches, like restaurants, hand out crayons and paper to youngsters as they enter. A child who is quietly coloring or drawing will rarely annoy her neighbors. Soft toys are good, and so are books. Do avoid anything noisy, though. The heads will whip around, for instance, if you hand your three-year-old your keys to play with and they fall on a stone floor.

No snacking.

If your child is ravenous or thirsty (or merely perceives this as a good ploy for alleviating boredom), exit. Few religious denominations will appreciate cracker crumbs on the velvet cushions.

Dress your children in quiet shoes.

Not necessary, of course, in mosques where shoes will be removed, or in carpeted buildings. But a mother did, once, bring a child in tap shoes to our church, which has tiled floors. She never returned.

Observe sartorial customs.

This requires a little research. Jewish males traditionally cover their heads as a sign of respect, while Christian men uncover theirs. Pants for women are still frowned on in some quarters, as are bare arms. Conservative congregations of any religion are more likely to observe these customs. If you are paying a visit to a new institution, find out ahead what is expected and prepare your child. The novelty of wearing a yarmulke or a lace mantilla can have considerable charm if it isn't sprung as a surprise on a balky four-year-old.

Ask if you're unsure about anything.

If you don't know whether your children should participate in part of the service, ask some friendly looking person nearby. Courtesy to newcomers should come with the territory.

Hospital Visits

Keep it short • Bring something for the patient. • Keep sick children at home • Children shouldn't make personal remarks about the patient • Children should try not to stare at other patients • Children shouldn't run or shout

Many hospitals place strict limits on child visitors, either because they view children as walking packages of potential infection (a pretty accurate view, if my kids represent the average) or because they consider kids disruptive to hospital routine. But there are times when either a patient or a child visitor will get a big charge out of a hospital visit, if it is planned right.

Keep it short.

Once a child has seen Mom in bed and understood that she's going to be fine and that squeaky, crunched-up baby in the wheeled cart is his new brother, Michael, there's not much more to be said. The cheering aspect of a hospital visit is the break in the monotony and the chance to keep emotional ties alive. When children are involved, this doesn't take very long.

Bring something for the patient.

You don't have to creep in disguised by an immense flower arrangement, but a bunch of grapes would probably come in handy, or a couple of magazines. If the patient is well enough, something your child can share with him, like a song tape or a pencil and paper game, is ideal.

Keep sick children at home.

The common cold would wreak havoc in an AIDS ward. A mild strep infection can spread like wildfire through a pediatric floor. At the faintest suspicion of a sniffle or a fever, postpone your hospital visit.

Children shouldn't make personal remarks about the patient.

You really can't censor a preschooler's conversation, but older children can be warned that the patient may look different or talk funny, and will almost certainly have on a weird looking nightgown. And that it's better not to mention these changes. And that you'll answer all the questions you can on the way home.

Children should try not to stare at other patients.

I know, it's like asking them not to breathe. But the fact is that when you take a healthy child to a hospital she's going to see people in wheelchairs and on gurneys or tottering along the hall, pushing an IV pole. It's confusing and scary and you don't want to overload your child with repressive restrictions. Try this: When you're prepping your child for the visit, warn him that a lot of people in the hospital aren't in very good shape. They probably wouldn't like to be stared at, because they get embarrassed. And leave it at that.

Children shouldn't run or shout.

People in hospitals sleep at strange times, and the staff always works very hard. Children pelting down halls and raising their voices disturb both work and rest, and undo the good that their visits bring in the first place.

Audience Participation

Choose an appropriate performance • Describe the
event beforehand • Be punctual • Dress your child
comfortably • Leave if you need to

In Part I, I gave some rules for taking children to live performances. Rules, that is, for how the children should behave. There's less of a chance that they'll disturb anyone else in the audience if you:

Choose an appropriate performance.

For small children, you'll be better off with performances specifically geared to the young. They'll be short, they'll include lots of visuals, and if there's a plot, it will be simple. Best of all, the entire audience will be twitchier than usual, so a little extra whispering from your youngster will be absorbed in the general noise. Preteens who are very interested in the arts can certainly enjoy performances aimed at adults. Younger kids probably would not.

Describe the event beforehand.

This is an important step for preschoolers, or for kids who aren't accustomed to live performances. Nobody likes to be unprepared. Tell your child about the concert hall, the seats in rows, the stage. The fact that she'll have to sit still. That she may not be able to see very well. That she won't be able to talk. Live theater is very different from movies, and you need to make that clear. Emphasize that you and she need to be unobtrusive so the performers can do their best.

Be punctual.

Allow more time than you think you'll need to get to the theater, find your seats, go to the bathroom, stroll around, go the bathroom again. Preschoolers always dig in their heels when you're in a hurry, and you don't want to have a battle of wills just before you ask your child to sit still for forty-five minutes.

Dress your child comfortably.

Of course you want to do justice to the situation by making your child presentable. But remember that new clothes are sometimes scratchy or distracting, which could make it hard to concentrate. Also remember that noisy accessories like charm bracelets or bangles will drive the people around you crazy.

Leave if you need to.

The foundation of teaching good manners to children is not asking too much of them. Maybe you're in a recital hall full of rapt six-year-olds, and your child seems to be the only one who is bored. She's starting to fidget and whisper and turn around in her seat to check out the rest of the audience. Face facts: This just doesn't interest her. Our son Willy has the attention span of a medieval scholar for any sports-related subject, but he couldn't care less about the arts. Rick took him to a musical last winter and Will was suffering through it with poor grace when he suddenly got sick to his stomach and had to be rushed out to the bathroom. He was pale green and shaky until he got into the cab coming home. The cab driver was listening to a hockey playoff game and Willy was instantly a new child. So we've learned our lesson. There is no point in taking him to a concert or a play at the moment. If your child shows signs of serious boredom, do yourself and everyone else a favor: Bail out. (A noisy moment in the show is the best time for a surreptitious exit.) You can always linger at the back of the hall to catch a few more minutes if your child suddenly perks up and takes an interest in the show. And remember, if you force a reluctant child to sit through a performance, you'll have to overcome that negative memory the next time you want to bring her along.

Traveling with Tots

Forget about table manners • Be extra nice to the flight attendants • Don't try to squeeze past the service carts • Take your child to the bathroom the minute the plane starts losing altitude to land

Whenever I start down the loading gate toward a plane, a paraphrase of Dr. Seuss's *Green Eggs and Ham* dances through my head: "Not in a car, not in a train, not on a bus, not in a plane. . . ." Please, no, not in a plane for six hours with small children. . . .

It doesn't help to know that the man behind me with the laptop computer and the garment bag is thinking the same thing.

But there we are, in forced intimacy, and I can only hope that I'll never see these people again, and that the children behave themselves. Which is largely my husband's and my responsibility.

I once had a rather pleasant conversation with a woman on a plane (this was in those far-gone days when the children would conk out for an hour or two). We were getting along fine, discussing books and her interesting life, which had included many cross-country trips with her children. "Of course in those days," she said, eyeing my immense and overflowing carry-on bag, "we didn't bring all the things for the children. They had to learn to entertain themselves, and eat whatever was available."

I didn't like her so much after she said that. Because that carry-on bag is a good part of the reason that the boys aren't wailing like banshees and running up and down the aisles of the plane, crashing into the beverage cart. The bag is full of food, water, books, crayons, tapes, cards, nasty little plastic army men, and heaven knows what else. I do, merely for form's sake, shove in a paperback of my own, but I rarely get to open it. I sometimes feel, when we touch down, as if I've spent six hours being a clown for an audience of two, but my husband says I'm exaggerating. And all this so that my children can try to be pleasant and courteous fellow travelers.

Keeping small children entertained is the first step toward this goal. The second step is not invading anyone else's personal space, a challenge when the airlines are allotting passengers less and less room as the years go by. This means not permitting your four-year-old to kick the seat back in front of her, and trying to prevent her from dropping Polly Pocket over the seat back behind her into somebody's microwaved lasagne.

Air travel permits some unusual freedoms, though, along with its constraints. If you take advantage of the former it may be easier to suffer the latter, and still have everyone beaming with approval rather than relief when you file out of the plane at the end of the trip.

Forget about table manners.

You didn't wear your new white jeans on the plane, did you? That was silly. You're going to function as a giant dish towel! Because your child is going to open every single one of those tiny little packages on the food tray and squeeze hard. And remember, airline salad dressing is *always* orange.

Be extra nice to the flight attendants.

You cannot say please and thank you enough to these hard-working people. Try to let them know that you understand they're run off their feet and that you deeply appreciate their efforts. If they know you're sympathetic, they will find the last can of apple juice on the plane for you.

Don't try to squeeze past the service carts.

On most newer planes, the aisles are too narrow. Time your excursions carefully for moments when the carts are in the galleys.

Take your child to the bathroom the minute the plane starts losing altitude to land.

The flight attendants don't want you out of your seat once the captain has said "Prepare for landing." If your child has not just been to the bathroom, this is when he will ask to go. If you absolutely, positively know that his bladder is empty it will be easier to keep him prisoner in his seat.

In all fairness I should say that it gets easier and easier to travel with my kids. But the experience of being imprisoned on a plane with a two-year-old has guaranteed that I will never again be one of those people who looks daggers at the little ones, trotting down the aisle with their backpacks.

Vacation Visits

I got a letter recently from a friend who lives in Mexico City. Her two teenage daughters had visitors for the Christmas vacation, girls they'd met at school in New York. Robyn wrote that the two guests were like Beauty and the Beast. One was enthusiastic and curious, willing to go along with the family's plans, interested in the culture of Mexico, ready to try the new foods, appreciative of Robyn's cooking, and helpful around the house. The other guest would eat nothing but cold cereal, dragged along moping on expeditions, got tired, missed her computer, and called home every night, telling her sister that she was having a terrible time.

The lesson for parents is this: Think very carefully before you accept an invitation for your child to visit another family in unfamiliar surroundings. You might have the most charming, easygoing son in the world, a boy who never interrupts and always helps with the dishes and writes ingenious thank-you notes. But he might not be a good traveler. Sometimes a sensitive, quiet child is overwhelmed by all the strangeness of a new place, and withdraws. Withdrawal often reads as sulkiness. And bang, everyone's unhappy: the guest, who just can't perk up, the host child, who won't be having much fun, and the host parent, who will loathe the sulky guest. Marvelous opportunities may come your child's way, but if you aren't sure that she can take them cheerfully in stride, it's better to say "No." It's also important to be frank about any of your child's characteristics that might be inconvenient on the trip planned. I have a friend who cannot tolerate cold. Her parents never took this condition seriously until she went on a ski weekend to Vermont with some friends and spent the entire three days in the ski lodge, playing solitaire and eating potato chips. A child who gets motion sick shouldn't go on a boat, and an asthmatic shouldn't stay with smokers.

On the other hand, if you do accept an invitation for your child, you have a couple of issues to work out. Money is one of them. When a family takes in another child, they spend extra money. So when you're discussing the trip with your child's friend's mother, ask "What do you think Luther's expenses will be? Can we contribute some money for gas and his meals?" You should let your child know what arrangements you've made, because by the age of nine or so they know that every ice cream cone or ticket to the water slide has to be paid for, and they may feel uncomfortably indebted if they don't know that you've already written a check. Be sure to give your child some pocket money, too, so that he can pay for his own souvenirs.

It would also be charming for your child to play host to the family that's hosting her, especially if she's spending more than a weekend with them. One way to do this is to trust your child with a sum of money that's earmarked for treating the host family to dinner in a restaurant or to several rounds of ice cream at the beach. You'll want to warn them that you've given Maxine this cash and she can either turn it over to the parents in charge or, if she's very confident, let her pay the bill at the restaurant. (Let her practice at least once with you, including counting the change and calculating the tip.)

And then, your child should also come bearing gifts. It's your job to pick out some appropriate offering, though you can ask for advice and shopping consultation if your child enjoys that kind of thing. If the gift reflects the occasion, so much the better: You could choose a couple of new board games for a trip to someone's country house, or a big bag of gourmet trail mix for a hiking trip.

Guests should also pitch in and help with chores. Your child wouldn't have been invited to join another family if the parents didn't think they'd enjoy her company. Obviously they believe (and you hope) that she won't be much trouble. It would be even nicer, though, if your child could volunteer to make one task her own. Maybe she's an early riser and could take charge of breakfast, or loves dogs and would be happy to feed and brush them. Or she could read the maps. I've heard about one boy who appointed himself official photographer, relieving the mother of the task and putting her in the vacation snapshots for once. He even put the best pictures in a little album and gave it to the family as a thank-you present. That's the kind of guest everyone wants to have!

RSVP

I know this is a book about teaching manners to children, but one of the reasons we spend time on this project is so that they will eventually be polite adults. And if they're going to be polite adults, you have to make sure they avoid making one of the most common and the most irritating manners mistakes going— not responding to an invitation.

It never fails. Ask any hostess. You send out 125 invitations to, say, a wedding. A good third of the potential guests will not respond. And some of them will actually have the nerve to show up at the reception anyway.

Don't let your child grow up into one of these delinquent guests. When he's very young, of course, you'll respond to all invitations for him. Around second grade, though, kids start making their own plans and sometimes they don't let the grown-ups know what these plans are. Kids call each other up with invitations and you might assume that just because Rashid told Lucas he was coming to Lucas's party, Lucas passed this information along to his mom. Well, maybe. And maybe not. The nice thing to do is to call and be sure the information got through. And if your child witnesses the call (and other calls like it), he'll realize that you think this party stuff is important. It wouldn't hurt if you pointed out that people need to know how many guests to expect so that there's enough food.

Your child may want to take over her own arrangements by the time she hits ten or twelve. When that time comes, you'll start asking, "Have you told Kyla yet that you're coming to her party? I'm sure her mom needs to know how many kids will be there." You might want to add, occasionally, that it's very rude for guests not to respond to invitations. You don't have to add that a lot of grown-ups have apparently never learned this lesson.

In Complex Families

The mother of one of Willy's friends is in the process of divorcing her husband. The whole affair is a sad tangle, and one of the factors that makes it difficult for young Robbie is that his father's standards of behavior are different from his mother's. One of the things they disagree about is manners. Robbie's father thinks that saying "Please" and "Thank you" represents the tyranny of an outmoded civilization. His mother merely thinks it's polite. So what is poor Robbie supposed to do? And how are parents supposed to teach their children manners when the children spend time in two or more different households, with different habits and priorities?

First, don't worry about manners if you're in crisis mode. There are times in everyone's life as a parent when getting food on the table, getting the kids off to school, and dispensing lots of affection are the priorities, and correcting behavioral quirks just doesn't happen. Often kids in a crisis are so frightened anyway that they wouldn't dream of acting up.

It's when you start to pick yourself up and put the pieces back together that you need to insist on a measure of courtesy. There are so many factors that may make this difficult: regression, regret, guilt, anger, and your children's constant testing of limits. But remember that they need structure, they need consistency, they need you to stand firm and insist that they be civil. You may not be moving foward and adding refinements of behavior at any great pace, but manners should still be part of the family curriculum when you're in charge.

I suppose that, in an incredibly civil situation, former spouses could share information on teaching manners, but I haven't seen any divorces like that among my friends. It's much more likely that one parent (the one who bought this book) places more emphasis on these skills.

Preschoolers, who are just becoming civilized, probably won't tax you with different standards. But a seven-year-old is very likely to say, "I don't have to clear my place at Dad's!" or "Mom doesn't bug me about saying please!" Stick to your guns. Your answer is, "Well, we do lots of things differently, don't we?" The fact that your child lives in two different households doesn't change your opinion about how often teeth need to be brushed. Manners are important, too. In fact if anyone needs social confidence and savoir faire, surely it's a child with a complicated family life.

Other People's Children

O nce you start expending energy on your own children's manners, you're bound to see some substantial improvements in their behavior. At the same time, though, you'll probably become aware of how many children fall short of the ideal. Sometimes parents who know I'm working on this book ask me questions like, "What can I do about a child who hangs up on me when I say my daughter's not at home?" or "What can I do about Martin's friend who never says please?"

The answer, I'm afraid, is, "Not a whole lot." Except take a deep breath and try to be understanding. The child who hangs up abruptly may be uneasy on the phone. The child who doesn't say please hasn't been taught that she should. Both children, as you now realize, are at a disadvantage in dealing with the world. They alienate and annoy people right and left. But it is not your business to fix this. Manners need to be taught with consistency by somebody who is around the child a great deal. An irritated grown-up issuing occasional instructions can't be of much help. So most of the time you're wasting your breath if you correct a child's behavior. In some circumstances, though, it's worthwhile.

If you see a great deal of a child, I think you can really have an impact on her behavior. Especially if she's in an eager-to-please phase. You make sure she knows what your household standards are: "In this house we leave our shoes at the front door, Zelda." Or "Do you see how Matthew is putting his juice cup in the sink?

Could you do that, too, please?" And then praise, praise, praise. Children who aren't yours are especially delighted to be told what they do right. A compliment to another adult, delivered in the child's hearing, is especially powerful. "Do you know, Marcus is the only boy who ever thanks me for bringing him home?"

Sometimes a child has an unmannerly habit that may drive you nuts. I have a lot of trouble with noisy eaters. I'll tolerate the smacking and chewing noises for a while, telling myself to cool off and not be such a crank. But if I start to get really worked up, I'll make a comment in a kindly tone of voice, like, "I know pizza is hard to eat, Joel, but could you chew with your mouth closed?" I've learned from experience that if I don't let off some steam this way I may say something nasty ten minutes later. If you have a short fuse about something, giving a child a gentle pointer is more constructive than repressing your annoyance and then blowing up.

Finally, children are sometimes unintentionally rude, and I think you do them a kindness to point this out as it happens. You can just say something like "Honey, it's rude to imitate somebody's accent. It hurts their feelings." You aren't really criticizing their behavior as much as you are handing them a piece of important information about how to stay on good terms with other people.

• S U L K I N G •

You can tell a child not to slam a door. You can tell him not to whine, not to sass you, and not to stick out his tongue. You cannot tell a child not to sulk.

Sulking is the invisible rebellion. You know your child is doing it: You can feel those waves of resentment rolling off of him, poisoning the air. But there's nothing you can actually put your finger on. Maybe that lower lip is sticking out a fraction of an inch. Maybe the shoulders are hunched a bit. Answers to your questions are certainly brief, and there's something draggy and reluctant about the way your sulky child does his chores. But there's nothing really obvious to remprimand.

That's the whole point. I am indebted to Miss Manners for pointing out, in *Miss Manners' Guide to Rearing Perfect Children*, that sulking is perfect behavior. And what your sulky child really wants more than anything is for you to challenge her. To say, "Stop sulking!" so she can say, "I'm not sulking!"

This is a power struggle of the subtlest kind. As a grown-up, you should win it. And the way to win is by ignoring the sulker. Continue to speak in a cheery voice. Pretend you're Donna Reed. Take the moral high ground, and remember, you have a longer attention span and more stamina. Before you know it, your sulker will have tucked in her lip and turned her attention to something more pleasant, and so can you.

A Final Note: Character Issues

I sometimes have a sinking feeling that parents are going to look at the suggestions (okay, rules) in this book and say to themselves, "Is she out of her mind? My kid would never do that!" and give up completely. "I could never get Zoe to stop interrupting." Or "Jake just *can't* sit still at the table for fifteen minutes."

Right. Nobody's perfect. I doubt that even Emily Post wrote a thank-you note for every present she ever received. And although my children are generally eager to please, there are areas where they don't even get close to the ideal.

Our children are all different, and they will fall short of perfection in ways that are dictated by their characters. An exuberant, intense child may ask more than his share of tactless questions—but this will also be the child who can be counted on to greet guests with lavishly affectionate interest. A thoughtful, reticent child may be monosyllabic with adults, but extremely sensitive about holding doors and carrying packages and giving up his seat on a crowded bus.

I'm not suggesting that you give up on teaching the lessons your child finds difficult. Quite the opposite: You should keep trying. All of us have areas in life where we could improve our behavior, and I think we should all still (yes, mature as we are) attempt to respond promptly to invitations and introduce ourselves to people who may not remember us.

But it's also important to recognize that your children and mine have their blind spots and they'll never behave perfectly. But if, by teaching manners, you manage to teach them respect and empathy for others and a little skill with the cutlery, you will have done them a great service.

Index

About the Author

Carol McD. Wallace is the author or coauthor of fifteen books, including *20,001 Names for Baby* and *The Official Preppy Handbook*. She is a frequent contributor to parenting magazines, and her column, "Modern Manners," ran in *Child* magazine for two years. She lives in New York City with her husband and two young sons.

11743266R00167

Made in the USA
San Bernardino, CA
26 May 2014